Perfected:

God's Best Reserved For You

A Study of Hebrews

Erynn Sprouse

My sweet husband has supported me completely as I have worked on this book and many other projects to God's glory. He is an excellent partner in marriage and even more so in ministry. While it is tempting to dedicate this book to him, I know he would rather it be now as it has been all along: dedicated to God's glory and the furtherance of His kingdom.

http://comefillyourcup.com

Finer Grounds / Perfected: God's Best Reserved For You

Published by Kaio Publications, Inc.
5008 Guardian Ct.
Spring Hill, TN 37174

ISBN: 978-0-9960430-2-1

Book edited by Erin McDonald

Design and layout: D.J. Smith, Nashville, TN

Printed in the United States of America.

Contents

About Erynn

Erynn Sprouse has been married to Jeremy since 1999. She earned her Associates from Adams State University and her Bachelor of Arts from Bear Valley Bible Institute of Denver. She is the creator and Editor of Come Fill Your Cup women's ministry, including website and retreats. She has enjoyed speaking for ladies' days and retreats in several states. She is a stay home, homeschooling mom to five boys and one girl in Dublin, Texas where Jeremy serves as the pulpit minister.

What is Finer Grounds?

Finer Grounds is a verse by verse, chapter by chapter, book by book, meaty, deep digging study of God's word. Enrich your personal Bible time or study with a group of ladies. Thought-provoking questions help you reach new levels of faith. Studies are thoroughly researched and passages are expertly explained. Lessons are structured in 13-week (one quarter) segments so you can easily share them with your ladies' Bible class.

Perfected: God's Best Reserved For You
A Study of Hebrews

From before the foundation of the world, God was planning for today, for this day of salvation, for this final age, and He saved the best for last. What He planned for the Israelites was amazing... but ultimately only a stepping stone to what He dreamt for us. In Hebrews, God's best, reserved for you, is revealed. What should our response be since we live in this privileged time? Join us as we journey through Hebrews and discover what the culmination of God's plans looks like and learn what it all means for us.

Chapter 1

Straight From the Horse's Mouth

Most introductions to books of the Bible begin with who wrote the book. But Hebrews is different from most books in many ways, one of which is that we don't really know who wrote it. Speculations abound, but whoever the author was, God did not see fit to preserve their name for us. Also, unlike many of our New Testament books, this is not an epistle or letter. Rather, it is an exhortation or sermon (cf. Hebrews 13:22). The writer declares the superiority of Jesus and Christianity over Judaism again and again, exhorting the reader to press on at all costs. To familiarize yourself with the book, try to read it in one sitting.

Read Hebrews 1:1-2.

Like most good sermons, Hebrews begins by jumping right into the subject matter in 1:1-2. God spoke long ago, the author asserts, and He has spoken in these last days. This latest declaration from God has come not by a prophet or even an angel, but via the Son of God Himself.

List characteristics of God's previous communication contrasted with that of "these last days":
To whom did God speak?
When did He speak?
What method did He use to communicate?

The fact that the message we have today came through the very Son of God makes it a superior message. In days gone by, God spoke to the fathers through visions, prophets and even Balaam's donkey. The message was in small portions and large portions. The message of Christianity, though, came from the very Heir of all things. It came over the course of Jesus' very brief lifetime and from those who learned the message from Him. The idea of the superiority of the second revelation over the first is the hub of the entire book of Hebrews. As we study, we will see that the writer continually proves the many ways God's message given through Jesus supersedes the revelation received by the fathers of the past, and how this fact demands whole-hearted, never-flinching perseverance.

Read Hebrews 1:2-4.

Here is one of the most amazing descriptions of Jesus I can think of in scripture. We see here a glimpse of who Jesus was and is. We see at least seven different aspects and acts of Jesus.

List five aspects/ acts of Jesus.

The phrase rendered "exact representation of His nature" in the New American Standard begins with a Greek word found only here in the New Testament. It is the word CARAKTER, where we get our word "character." It's a word used of coinage, stamps and seals. When you ink a stamp, you cover the rubber part with ink and press it to paper, leaving behind an impression that exactly matches the image on the stamp. When the U.S. Mint creates a coin, the small metal disc goes through a long and precise process before it is deemed worthy of circulation; it must meet all the standards and look exactly as it should before it can represent the government of the United States as currency. Here the Hebrews writer describes Jesus using a term which conveys the same idea. He is exactly the message and perfect representation of Yahweh God Himself (this is also the idea expressed in John 1:1-14 by calling Jesus the "Word").

Which description of Christ's acts/aspects stands out to you or means the most to you? Why?

Read Hebrews 1:5-9.

The Hebrews writer introduces a primary reason Jesus is superior to the angels: He is the Son (note: a careful reading of the original context of these quotes [Psalm 2:7; Samuel 7:14] shows that "son" is more than a term for offspring, but also a term for the anointed ruler or king. We will not discuss this aspect here, but it is an interesting study). Paradoxically, the Son is also God. The word translated "worship" in verse six is PROSKUNEO, and it refers to the kind of worship only God should receive (cf. Luke 4:8).

Read Acts 10:25, 26.

What does Peter do when Cornelius worships at his feet?

Read Revelation 22:8, 9.

Who did John attempt to worship? Whom is he told he should worship?

Fill in the blanks (note: version used here is NASB, but all reliable translations render the words for the blanks the same):

Hebrews 1:8

"But of the _____ He says, "Your throne, O _____ is forever and ever, and the righteous scepter is the scepter of His kingdom."

The fact of Christ's deity is undeniable in this passage of scripture and gives further weight to the message He delivered. The same line of thought is continued to verse 13.

Read Hebrews 1:13, 14.

Sitting at the right hand indicates high authority. To be at the right hand is to be second in command. The angels, however, are ministering spirits whose job it is to minister to the recipients of salvation, that is, to us. So why all this discussion on angels? The Hebrews writer wraps up the topic in 2:1-3a.

Read Hebrews 2:1-4.

Here's where the rubber meets the road, so to speak. So Jesus is greater than the angels. So He's God. So... what does that mean for me? The Hebrews writer is about to answer that question.

The "word spoken through angels" refers to the first revelation-- the one spoken to the fathers (cf. 1:1). We read that it was unalterable or steadfast and that every instance of breaking the laws of that revelation was met with a punishment. Yet what we have today is so much greater that it was delivered by the Son of God Himself... God's firstborn, the very radiance of His glory, the one through whom all things were made, He who made purification for sins, who sits at the right hand of the Father... God in the flesh. Not only was this message spoken through the Lord, but it was also confirmed by those who walked with Him. God Himself also confirmed their message by providing power for signs and wonders via the miraculous workings of the Holy Spirit.

Read Matthew 23:23.

Here Jesus is having yet another round with the scribes and Pharisees. They have been careful in all the small things and paid close attention, but they have neglected the larger matters of justice, mercy and faithfulness. Interestingly, He does not condemn them for carefully tithing the mint and dill and cummin. In fact, He comes about as close to praising them as He ever does in the New Testament. Jesus tells them they should have been careful in these matters of tithing and in the large matters of justice, mercy and faithfulness.

The Hebrews writer's point in 2:1-4 is that if under the old covenant, they were right in being as careful as the scribes and Pharisees were, how much more careful must we be? The writer encourages us to "pay much closer attention," admonishes us not to drift away, and warns us again about neglecting so great a salvation. Drifting and neglecting are not conscious acts. They are sneaky; they creep up slowly over time if one is not careful, diligent, if one is not paying attention. We must be conscientious to devote time to study, to prayer, and to good works (Ephesians 2:10).

SIDE STUDY

Hebrews 1:3, 4 is an excellent text to explain the purpose of signs, wonders and miracles. The reason God's will allowed for them was to confirm what was being said of Him in the messages preached by the apostles and others with the gifts of the Holy Spirit. Today, if I want to know whether the preacher is speaking truth or not, I simply pull out my Bible and check out what he's saying. In the times before the Bible was completed, though, what could be done? If the preacher could perform a miracle-- an act that only God could do—it was like God saying, "Yes, what He's saying is true. I'm with him." 1 Corinthians 13:8-13 poetically refers to the times of the gifts of prophesy and tongues and miraculous knowledge as being "partial." In that passage, Paul says those gifts will pass away when the "perfect" or complete comes; that is, when the full revelation has come, miraculous gifts will cease. They will no longer be needed, but faith, hope, and love will be needed yet. Consider also what Jesus says in John 5:36. The works, or miracles, that Jesus was doing testified that He had been sent by God. Likewise, for those who heard Jesus' message and confirmed it to others, God again testified on their behalf by miracles (Hebrews 1:3,4). Today, since we have their message recorded in written form, there is no need for miracles or signs or wonders. We can verify the Bible as the word of God with thorough investigation.

Chapter 2
The Ultimate Sacrifice

If you haven't done so yet (or even if you have), try to make time to read the book of Hebrews-- beginning to end-- in one sitting. It can seem like a daunting task, but remember this is how the recipients would likely have gotten the text. Reading it this way enables you to more easily see the big picture. If you find it hard to focus, try listening to an audio recording of the Bible as you read. There are many free recordings available online. Just so you know, it takes the average reader 26 minutes to read the book of Hebrews (source: http://www.housetohouse.com/HTHPubPage.aspx?pub=2&issue= 673&section=756&article=4862). Not too bad!

Read Hebrews 2:5.

There is a cutesy saying in hermeneutics (the study of... well... of how to study your Bible) that if you see a "therefore," you need to find out what it's there for. The same goes for "for" in the case of Hebrews 2:5. Here the Hebrews writer is continuing a discussion begun in 1:10 regarding the world to come: it was subjected to Jesus, not to angels. This fact further shows His superiority to angels, and thus, the superiority of His message to that of the message spoken through them (2:2).

Read Hebrews 2:6-9.

The Hebrews writer says "... one has testified somewhere..." The "one" is David and the "somewhere" is Psalm 8 (note: this isn't the Hebrews writer having a brain bubble and not being able to remember who said what where. Remember that these are inspired scriptures. We can't say for sure why the writer didn't record the specific "who" and "where," but we also cannot say the writer was forgetful).

Read Psalm 8.

I can almost see David out on his balcony, looking up at the stars and feeling all his smallness in the universe. He wonders who he is, in comparison to God and His works, that the Creator of all should pay him any mind. In Hebrews 2, this same idea is applied to Jesus-- the same Jesus who now upholds all things by the word of His power (1:3). This Jesus came to earth and was made by God a little lower- less in power- than the angels. He became just as small as David felt, lived the life of a poor man and died the death of a criminal. After His death, He was crowned with glory and honor, and all things were put in subjection to Him.

Read 1 Corinthians 15:21-28.

The apostle Paul lays out a sort of timeline for us here. Death came by a man (Adam), and all have the opportunity to be made alive through another man, Christ. Christ suffered death, was made alive, then when He returns, His followers will also be made alive. At that time, He will hand over the kingdom (read: church, cf. Daniel 2:44) to the Father. Also at that time, all authority and power will be abolished.

Who/what is the last enemy to be abolished?

All things are subjected to Christ except _____.

Will Christ ever be subjected? If so, when and to whom?

The Hebrews writer points out that all things have been put into subjection to Christ, but the complete fulfillment of this has not yet happened. While we do not yet see all things subjected (namely, death is not yet subject), we do see Christ crowned with glory, seated at the right hand of the Majesty on high and no longer lower than the angels (1:3, 4).

SIDE STUDY:

The literalist in me struggles to understand the idea that all things are subject to Christ, yet not all things are subject. Something that helps me is to think of Joseph in Egypt when he interprets Pharaoh's dream and becomes second in command. Scripture records Pharaoh saying, "See, I have set you over all the land of Egypt" (Genesis 41:41). In the previous verse, he explains that Joseph will be over Pharaoh's house and all the people will pay homage, and the only thing that will not be under Joseph's authority is the throne itself. Does that mean Pharaoh contradicted himself when he said Joseph would be over all Egypt? Of course not. We understand intuitively that the one who gives the authority cannot be under that same authority.

It is likewise with Jesus. All authority has been given to Him in Heaven and on Earth (Matthew 28:18). God the Father who gave the authority is obviously not under the authority. Jesus also has authority over death--this was demonstrated in His resurrection-- but the full subjection will not happen until His second coming, for which God patiently awaits, allowing maximum time for repentance (2 Peter 3:9). I liken this to a trust fund. If the trust fund is in Joe Schmoe's name, it is his. However, it is not subjected to him until he is of age or he meets whatever stipulations that have been made.

In the case of Christ, death is His. It has been conquered, but the full subjection will not come until the end of days. 1 Corinthians 15:28 reveals the final stage of God's plan: once all things, including death, have been subjected, Christ will hand over the kingdom to God, having fulfilled His mission. This is the same thing as if Pharaoh had told Joseph he would be second in command until the famine was over. At the end of the 14 total years, Joseph would have returned the signet ring and all that had been accumulated during his time of authority. Jesus has all authority only until the end of the age. When He returns and death is finally subjected, the Bible says that God will be all in all, a strong phrase referring to the complete supremacy that will be God's upon all enemies, including death, being no more. Christ's subjection is directly tied to our need for a perfect high priest who is alone qualified as the book of Hebrews points out later. This helps us to more fully appreciate the sacrifice-- both temporal and eternal-- that Christ made on our behalf.

Read Hebrews 2:10-13.

Christ's mission was to _____ (cf. 2:10).

In order to accomplish this mission, Jesus needed to become perfect (note: the word translated in the NASB as "perfect" is one which means to complete or bring to completion[1]; this kind of perfection does not necessarily refer to flawlessness, though we know Christ was also that). What He needed in order to be complete for His mission was experience with suffering.

"Sanctify" is not typically in our every day vocabulary, but it basically means to be made morally clean. It is as though, in a moral sense, our sins made us filthy. Imagine a homeless man on the street who has not bathed in weeks upon weeks, and he is about to meet the king. Before that happens, he needs to be washed and groomed. But we are not mere beggars pulled in off of the streets. No, Jesus is our brother! "What a privilege to be called brothers of the Son of God! He who is seated at the right hand of the Majesty in heaven condescends to sinful man and unashamedly calls him brother" (Matt. 28:10; John 20:17).[2] What a privilege indeed, and not one to be claimed without backing. The Hebrews writer provides three scriptures to support his claim of kinship.

Read Hebrews 2:14.

If Christ was to suffer and die, He would need a body, so he became flesh and blood (cf. John 1:14). The point was to render

Satan powerless by removing his source of power, by taking out his greatest weapon.

Read 1 Corinthians 15:53-57.

Fill in the blanks:

The _____ of death is _____ and the power of _____ is the _____ (1 Cor. 15:56).

Read Romans 7:7-8 and Colossians 2:13-14.

The Law was the power of sin, the very thing that stood as the standard of accusation. But Christ, through His death, removed it, nailing it to the cross. It no longer stands there to point out every failing, and because of His death, because of His sacrifice, we who are in Christ are marked righteous.

Read Hebrews 2:15.

Because of Christ's victory over death, the Christian is able to essentially laugh at death. "What are you going to do? Kill me? Go for it. I'd love to go to Heaven." Paul welcomed death and saw it as a gain (Philippians 1:21). Death holds no fear for the Christian.

Read Hebrews 2:16.

The Hebrews writer gives a nod back to his previous argument. He has just been explaining that Jesus cares so much for us that He is not ashamed to call us brethren and even took on mortal flesh.

Such help is not even extended to angels, but only to Abraham's descendants (cf. Galatians 3:26-29).

Read Hebrews 2:17-18.

God had a problem. The crown of His creation, mankind, the object of His heart's desire was out of His reach. Like a parent whose child has sunken into the depths of a drug-addicted life on the streets, He longed to bring His beloved back to Himself, back to glory. But He could not navigate those streets Himself. The parent of a drug-addicted child sends someone familiar with street life to find and reclaim their child. But God had no such person to turn to. So Jesus stepped in. He gave up His claims to deity and forsook His Heavenly home. He came to earth and became familiar with the streets and the life mankind lives on them. He faced the same temptations that mankind faced. He endured the same trials. He suffered in the flesh and blood He had adopted. But suffering was not sufficient by itself. His death was required. Unjustified though it was, His death was necessary. And so He suffered, then died. And in so doing, He became the one for God to turn to. He became the go-between, showing God's beloved the way home. Christ became what mankind could not, and what God so desperately wanted. He became our way home, our way off the streets and back to the loving arms of our waiting Father. He stands today at the right hand of the Father, having paid the price for sin, having removed the standard of accusation, and He continually helps those who God so completely loved that He gave all He had to bring them home.

Chapter 3
Confidence Required

Reminder: try to read through the book of Hebrews in one sitting. Really. It will help you get the overall message. This week, as you read through the book, watch for and take note of warnings about the possibility of losing salvation. Now, let's dive in!

Read Hebrews 3:1.

Remember that when we see a "therefore" we need to find out what it's there for. The Hebrews writer is referring back to the fact that Jesus came, was tempted, suffered and died, thus is able to understand our struggles, relate to us, and help us.

The writer refers to the reader in two ways: "holy brethren" and "partakers of a heavenly calling." This will become important down the road as we see warnings of the possibility of losing one's salvation. Some contend that it is not possible, and argue that those who appear to fall away were never really "of" the faith. Affectionate, inclusive terms like the Hebrews writer uses belie this idea.

The writer encourages us to "consider Jesus, the Apostle and High Priest of our confession." There's a lot there! To consider is to mull something over, to think extensively and perhaps even intensively about it. Here we're asked to consider Jesus. Specifically, we're to consider him as an Apostle. An apostle is someone who is sent with a purpose as a representative. Jesus was God's representative. He carries the authority of the One who sent Him. This has bearing on the message He brought and how we receive it.

We're also asked to consider Jesus as the High Priest of our confession. The idea of Christ as the High Priest is one we'll be focusing more on later. For now, let's focus on the idea of our confession. When we want to understand what a word means, the best way to do that is to look at it in different contexts. Just as children learn what words mean by hearing them used in various ways in sentences, we can better understand what a word means by observing it in use. When we're talking about Bible words, it's most useful to stick with one book and/or writer. Other books can give us clues, but we want to draw our main definition from the same author or book. If you want to understand why better, study the idea of "works" in Romans and in James.

Read Hebrews 3:1, 4:14, 10:23.
Define confession:
Read Hebrews 3:2-6.

Christ has already been shown as superior to angels, and now we will see His superiority to Moses. This will again reinforce Jesus' message as one that eclipses all others. If Jesus is superior to the writer of the first five Old Testament books, then His message is also superior. The comparison centers on God's house. Both were faithful, but filled different roles.

Read Hebrews 3:3, 4.

Moses is worthy of glory, but not nearly as much as Jesus. Moses was a member of the house, but Jesus is the very builder. Suppose for a moment that a famous architect is inside one of his buildings as it catches on fire. Will the firemen be more concerned with rescuing the architect or in putting the flames out so as to salvage the building? Of course, the person will receive the greatest attention. Likewise Jesus receives more honor than that which He has built.

Read Hebrews 3:5, 6.

Moses' role was to create a testimony for later generations. He likely had no idea of the significance of Melchizidek or the correspondence that would be drawn between God's son and the priesthood, but he was faithful in his task. Christ, though, was faithful as a son. A faithful servant is a blessing, but only insomuch as he/she enables the employer to accomplish what needs done. The real honor, then, goes to the employer— in this case, God and His son.

Complete the chart:

Position's in God's House

Jesus		Moses	
	(vs 3)	Member	(vs 2)
	(vs 6)	Servant	(vs 5)

Read Hebrews 3:6.

Here we have the first hint of what will become a theme of the book: warnings that it is possible to fall away and lose one's salvation. If you are a Bible marker, chose a color or a symbol to mark the warnings found in the book of Hebrews. I chose a red exclamation point with a triangle around it as my symbol and drew it in the margin beside each such warning. The warnings are not worded in one, consistent way, so you'll have to be on the lookout. In this chapter, there are warnings in 3:6, 12.

Fill in the blank:

"...Whose house we are, _____ we _____ our confidence and the boast of our hope firm until the end" (3:6b).

"Hold fast," in modern times, is a term sailors use for a rope or line that is firmly and positively secured. Sailors used to tattoo "hold fast" on their hands, one letter per finger so that when they held two fists together, the phrase could be read. They superstitiously believed that the tattoo would help keep their hands from slipping on wet ropes. It provides us a picture of a sailor holding on to the riggings of his ship as a storm blasts on all sides, wind whipping waves over the edge of the rails. He holds fast, come what may. The Hebrews writer tells us that we must hold fast—really take hold and hang on— to our confidence and the boast of our hope, not just today, not just for a while, but until the end.

Take a moment to pray that God will help you hold fast to your confidence and boast of hope, just as the sailor holds fast.

SIDE STUDY:

Confidence through Christ

There is an idea in the religious world that we must always be in mind of our sinfulness and unworthiness to be called God's child. You may well find men and women of faith all but groveling in prayer. These same men and women refer to the blood-washed brethren of Christ as sinners. Is this really the way God would have us to be?

The word for confidence occurs four times in the book of Hebrews. We are expected to hold onto our confidence in 3:6. In 4:16, we are told to draw near to the very throne of God with confidence. 10:19 claims that we can confidently enter the Holy of Holies. Further down in the chapter, we are assured that our confidence has a great reward (10:35).

It is not God's intention for us to be constantly reminded that our place in His house is not an earned one. He has given it and done so freely. Once we have become partakers of the heavenly calling, we share in Christ's reward. Rather than continually pricking ourselves about sinful pasts, God would have us know that our forgiven sins are as far as the East is from the West (Psalm 103:12). He would have us approach Him in prayer and worship confidently. In fact, He demands that we do so. Hebrews 3:6 explains that we are Christ's house if and when we hold fast to this confidence which God has granted us.

Read Acts 4:13.

What was the source of the disciples' confidence?

"Boast of our hope," as the NASB translates this phrase, can also be rendered "rejoicing of the hope" as the KJV and NKJV have. Hope and confidence go hand in hand. If you are confident of your position in God's household, you must also maintain hope of salvation, to such a point that you take pride in it. A child who is sure their Christmas present will be a bike may go around boasting of his coming gift to his friends. In his mind, the bike is already his. Likewise, our hope, our salvation, is already ours and should be our pride and joy. This hints at evangelism, too. Hope held in secret lacks confidence. It is more of a fond wish than true hope. True hope is solid, unwavering, and it overflows to others.

Read Hebrews 3:7-11.

Quoting from Psalm 95, the Hebrews writer reminds us that there are already those who have failed to attain the rest and reward God offered.

Read Hebrews 3:12, 13.

Here we find our second warning, but not a warning alone. Verse 13 offers a way to help our brethren not to fall away.

What does the Hebrews writer tell us to do to keep the deceitfulness of sin from hardening our hearts?

What, specifically, will you do today and tomorrow to encourage your brethren? Make a plan including a time to

carry out your plan. Mark it in your calendar and be sure to follow through!

Read Hebrews 3:14.

What two verses from this chapter does this verse sound like?

Repeated words and phrases often highlight a key thought. We've had two chapters expressing the supremacy of Christ and here we have a promise that we are partakers of Him! What a promise!

Read Hebrews 3:15-19.

Read Numbers 14:6-11; 22-35 (if you are not familiar with the story of the ten spies, read all of Numbers 13, 14).

Hebrews 3:18 says that those who did not enter God's rest were disobedient. How so?

Read Hebrews 3:18,19.

Here disobedience and unbelief are equated. We learn that not believing is the same as doing something that is flat-out wrong.

What, specifically, did the Israelites not believe?

What is it that we are to believe and to hold fast as expressed in this chapter?

Hope is not hope if it wavers. Hope stands confidently in the face of all that might assail it. If my husband asks me to do something for him, he does not come and check up on me to make sure I've done it. He trusts me to do what I said I would do. Likewise, we must trust that when we obeyed the gospel and became partakers of the heavenly calling, the hope we had then will be met by God. We must also understand that God expects us to maintain that hope confidently, assuredly, to the very end. He is a God of justice who will keep His word, including the promise that those who succumb to unbelief will not enter His rest.

Chapter 4

Reward for the Faithful of the Great High Priest

Make it your aim to read through the book of Hebrews in one sitting again for this lesson and as you do, watch for references to the reward promised to those who remain faithful. If you are a Bible marker, you may want to mark these in your margin in a particular way. A couple of suggestions would be to draw a present or a cloud (to represent Heaven).

Also, notice (and mark, if you like) the many references to Jesus being the high priest. In the NASB, there are 18 occurrences. The idea of Jesus as a high priest mediating between God and man would have meant quite a lot to the original readers of this exhortation. It's a two-fold illustration. First, it explains the relationship we have with Him (part of the relationship, anyway). Second, it tells these Christians who are considering abandoning their faith that the highest position of the Jewish faith now belongs to Jesus; there is no other valid way.

Read Hebrews 4:1, 2.

This "therefore" refers back to the previous chapter and the lesson to be learned from the Israelites. Though they had a promise of entering the Promised Land, they fell short and died in the wilderness because of their unbelief (equated with disobedience in 3:18). Here we find yet another of the Hebrews writer's warnings against falling away, falling short, losing our salvation.

Though the people who followed Moses out of Egypt and into the desert may seem like little more than characters in a story to us and to the recipients of this letter, we find that we have more in common than first meets the eye. They had a promise of rest and the promise remains. They had good news (same word as "gospel") preached to them and so have we. But this is where the Hebrews writer warns us we'll want the similarities to end. The Israelites did not believe the promises.

What was it the Israelites weren't willing to do? What faith were they lacking? They weren't willing to press on in the face of difficulty. The people of the land they'd been promised seemed too big. The problems ahead, the hurtles between where they stood and their goal seemed insurmountable. They gave up, gave in, threw in the towel. What about us? When we're faced with struggles and temptations in life, sometimes it seems like too much. We cry out to God, "Why me? How much more, God?" And some become disobedient. Their attendance in the assembly becomes sporadic and then only a memory. Their prayers become feeble, and their hearts drift. These people, though we love them, will not enter God's rest. The hearing of the word is not met with faith, for faith is enduring. There is only one rest remaining, and we must fear lest we come short.

Read Hebrews 4:3-5.

Who will enter God's rest?

Those who believe enter God's rest, but those who do not believe (remember belief and obedience have been equated) push God to wrath, and He will not allow them to enter the rest He has had planned since the foundation of the world.

Just as in 2:6, the Hebrews writer sounds as though he can't put his finger on just where that scripture is.

"Some have understood this as proof the writer was not inspired. However, they have failed to understand the culture in which this type of terminology was used. This is a literary device characteristic of ancient writers, and was often used to draw special attention to the quote. In addition, this implies that his readers already knew where the passage could be found (in this case it is Genesis 2:)."[3]

God set up the principle of a rest in the very beginning. He continued the concept when He commanded the Israelites to observe the Sabbath. We know how wonderful it is to enjoy a day off after a long week of work. Such a rest is small potatoes compared to the rest that waited for the Israelites in the Promised Land and not even a speck in comparison to the rest that waits those who believe today.

Read Hebrews 4:6-9.

The Hebrews writer uses David's psalm as evidence that a rest remains. David wrote a number of years after the Israelites initially failed to take the promised land, yet he encourages his readers not to harden their hearts "today." There must, then, be another rest remaining. Since David was likely writing from the then-conquered Promised Land (delivered by Joshua), and is writing of another day of rest to come, there must remain a Sabbath rest for the people of God.

SIDE STUDY:

In Numbers 13 and 14, the Israelites had a promise of rest. They had the promised land before them. They spied out the land and saw that it was great... but they also saw the giants they'd have to defeat... and their hearts sank, they gave up, and the Hebrews writer says they were disobedient (3:18). They pushed God to wrath and He swore they would not enter that rest. We can't spy out Heaven, but we, too, have a promise of rest. We can't see the amazing things God has planned for us, but sometimes we do see the giants standing in our way... and sometimes those giants cause us to lose hope, and weigh down our hearts.

It seems we all know someone who was once part of the fold, but has drifted away. Think for a few moments, and take down a few notes. What happened? What giant did they see? Was there some stress in their life that influenced their move away from God? (She's been gone ever since her divorce... They went through foreclosure... Their daughter was in a wreck...).

Now pray. Pray for that person that his or her heart will not be hard, but will be softened.

Caleb spied out the land, and he saw how great it was. He saw the giants, but he knew his God was bigger. Forty-five years later, Caleb took the mountain he'd set his eyes on when he first arrived (Joshua 14:6-15). Seeing the giants doesn't have to mean losing hope, losing faith, and falling into disobedience.

It seems we all know someone who has faced down giants in their life. What could have shipwrecked their faith didn't. What could have caused them to lose hope now stands as a reason they hope all the more. Write down a few notes about one of these giant slayers you've known.

Now pray. Pray for that person and thank God for the influence they have and the example they've been.

Read Hebrews 3:12-14.

What can you do TODAY to encourage both of these people? Can you write a note? Make a phone call? Give a hug? Figure out what you can do, and do it.

Read Hebrews 4:10.

The sluggard does not earn a day off. He has not worked, so from what would he rest? God worked for six days to create the Universe and then rested on the seventh day. We have had the good news preached to us and now must unite that word with faith and work! Only when we have entered God's rest will we rest from our works.

Use a concordance to find other verses about work and the Christian by searching for "works" (note: if you do not have an exhaustive concordance, you can find one on BlueLetterBible. org). By the way, if you haven't used a concordance before, don't be overwhelmed. It's basically an index for the Bible. Easy as a dictionary to use!

List one verse from Ephesians and one from James here.
Can a Christian who is not active in their faith be saved?

Read Hebrews 4:11.

We have an example here of an "hortatory subjunctive." Unless you're a grammar geek (nothing wrong with that!), you probably haven't heard of that before. Basically, it's a command wearing nicer, more polite clothes. When I tell my children, "Let's get that bedroom clean!" it's a command. They need to get that bedroom clean, but it sounds nicer to say "Let's..." than to simply demand they get the job done. The Hebrews writer is a fan of the hortatory subjunctive, and they're sprinkled 13 times throughout the book. If you are a Bible marker, you may want to circle, underline, color or otherwise mark these.

There are four "let us" commands in Hebrews 4.
List them here:
1)
2)
3)
4)

Here we are commanded to be "diligent" as the NASB and NKJV translates it. Other reliable versions have "make every effort," "strive," "labor" (NRSV, ESV, KJV, respectively). We also find this word in 2 Peter 1:10.

Read 2 Peter 1:10,11.

What command does Peter give?

Read Hebrews 4:12, 13.

These verses are often quoted because they paint quite a picture of God's word, but what purpose do they serve here in the context of Hebrews? The writer again warns the reader that these promises, both of reward and punishment, are not mere dead words. No, they are living, active, and sharp. Following the example of disobedience (4:11) will result in a fall, and such a one will most certainly not enter God's rest.

Read Hebrews 4:14-16.

I don't know about you, but to know that "all things are laid bare to the eyes of Him with whom we have to do" is a scary thought. I'm not perfect, and if my entering that rest is based on my own merit and works, I'm sunk. The Hebrews writer here offers assurance to me and to other imperfect people. Jesus the Son of God, my great high priest, passed through the heavens and sympathizes with my weaknesses. More than that, He has been tempted just as I am daily tempted, and He didn't fall prey. He remained sinless and has paved the way to the throne of grace. Because of Him, I can draw near to that throne. More than that. I am commanded to draw near, not in a cowering manner, not in fear of judgment, but to draw near with confidence. There I receive mercy and grace to help in my struggles and temptations.

Read Hebrews 4:14-5:4

Here we once again see Christ as a high priest and discuss the idea further. The characteristics of an earthly high priest parallel Christ in many ways.

Earthly High Priest	Jesus the High Priest
Appointed on behalf of men (5:1)	He is our great high priest (4:15)
Offers gifts and sacrifices for sins (5:1)	Offered once for all time (10:12)
Beset with weaknesses (5:2)	Sympathizes with our weaknesses, tempted in all things (4:15)
Offers sacrifices for himself as well as the people (5:3)	Without sin (4:15)
Called by God (5:4)	Glorified by God to the post (5:5-6)

The high priest is one who—as a man who struggles with his own weaknesses—can understand his fellows, yet is appointed by God to serve, offering gifts and sacrifices for sins, thus building a bridge between man and God.

Read Hebrews 5:5-6.

This is the second time the Hebrews writer has quoted Psalm 2:7 (cf. Hebrews 1:5). We have noted previously that the term "son" refers to more than lineage in God's word. Guy Orbison explains, "That Christ is pre-existent is without question (John 1:15, 8:58, and 17:5). Therefore, this cannot mean that He is Son in the sense of being physically born. In His resurrection and ultimate ascension, He was crowned king. 'Son' is the relationship the Israelite kings sustained with God (see 2 Samuel 7:14)."[4]

Psalm 110:4 is quoted here, one which must surely have confused many over the years. The Hebrews writer's coming explanation of what this means is considered by many a mark of inspiration. In context, the point the writer is making is that not only is Jesus the king, as ordained by God, but He is also the high priest, also as ordained by God. Only God could do this since under the Old Testament kings and priests came from different tribes. Priests were of the family of Levi (high priests were specifically of Aaron's lineage), while kings came from the family of Judah. Under this system, it was impossible for one person to be both high priest and king.

Read 1 Samuel 13:8-14.

What happened when King Saul took on a priestly duty?

Read Hebrews 5:7, 8.

What happens when my son and I want different things? I want him to go do his school work. He wants to go play outside. Who will win? If he is an obedient son, I win, and the school work gets done. What happens when we want the same thing? He's anxious to go play outside and I'm anxious for him to get some exercise and expend some energy. Out he goes, and we both win, but there isn't necessarily any obedience involved. So it was with Christ in the Garden of Gethsemane and during his following torture and crucifixion.

Read Mark 14:32-39.

Record Jesus' prayer from Mark 14:36 here:

How many times did He pray this?

Read Mark 14:40-15:37, and write down as many things as you can that He suffered. Don't worry about getting everything down; but do consider his physical, emotional and spiritual sufferings.

Christ knew what was coming when He prayed in the Garden. In Luke's account, we read that an angel came and strengthened Him, yet He was still under such stress that his sweat fell like drops of blood (Luke 22:41-44). Hebrews 5:7 tells us that He was heard, yet God's answer in this case was "No." Though God could have saved Him from death, He allowed His Son to suffer, and Christ, in obedience to the Father, accepted the suffering. "To ask to be saved from death and then to give oneself over to death as did Jesus would bring the full force of obedience to one's experience."[5]

Read Hebrews 5:9-10.

You may be thinking, "Christ became perfect? But I thought He was already sinless..." Jesus was certainly not in need of any makeover. The word translated "perfect" here is the Greek word TELEIOO. It means to be made complete, to reach a desired end, to fulfill something or to overcome an imperfect state. Since we know Jesus was not imperfect, it's clear that the other definitions fit better. In His perfecting, Jesus became the savior He came to earth to be as well as the high priest "according to the order of Melchizedek."

This idea of the order of Melchizedek must have been one of great curiosity, but the writer isn't quite ready to reveal what he means. First, he has something to say about how the brethren are doing.

Read Hebrews 5:11-14.

"Dull of hearing," lazy, sluggish. No one appreciates a lazy or sluggish worker, and this is not how a Christian should be either, yet this is the description used of the Hebrews. He says that they should be teachers by now. They should have grown past the point of needing to be spoon-fed and should be capable enough to teach. Instead, they need someone to teach them the very basics, the most fundamental parts of God's word. The writer further compares the readers to babies who cannot yet even eat table food.

"For everyone who partakes only of milk is not accustomed to the word of righteousness, for he is an infant." Did you know that if one stops consuming meat for long enough, the stomach will stop producing the acids required for their digestion? Similarly, when we fail to challenge ourselves in learning God's word, we begin to find difficulty in understanding. There are Christians who have been sitting in church pews for decades yet can barely understand much beyond the most basic of teachings. What a shame!

"Solid food," the Hebrews writer continues, "is for the mature." The word translated "mature" is TELEIOS. Does that look familiar? These Christians are still on milk when they should be on solid food. They should be mature— this is the designed end! We are imperfect, but we should be continually overcoming this imperfect state! We must constantly strive to grow and mature, handling solid food and even "meat." By doing so, we train ourselves, our senses, our consciences to discern good from evil.

Chapter 5
Beware of Complacency

Again, I want to encourage you to read through the entire book of Hebrews in one sitting. We have previously noted the many occurrences of warnings in the book, but this time let's look at what makes those warnings necessary. This week as you read through the book of Hebrews, notice what sins, difficulties, or behaviors could precipitate losing one's salvation.

Read Hebrews 5:11-6:8.

This is a longer chunk than we usually look at in one piece, and we'll be breaking it down further, but it's important to understand that this is all one thought. I was amazed in studying this chapter to see that the Hebrews writer's admonition against their lack of maturity is directly connected to one of the strongest warnings we have in all of scripture about the possibility of falling away. I don't know how many times I've looked at this passage and either stopped after 6:3 or started at 6:4. Somehow, until studying this passage for this lesson, I had never connected these verses. What a lesson I've been missing! The Hebrews writer is warning his readers that their lack of growth puts them in a position where they are in danger of falling away, crucifying their Savior again and putting Him to open shame. In verse 8, he warns that like ground yielding thorns and thistles, they are close to being cursed and then burned.

Typically we talk about the need for growth in one's spiritual life as something we really ought to do, much like we really ought to eat healthy food instead of chowing down on doughnuts, and we really ought to get to the gym more often. We know we ought to, but we're not going to, and we know it.

In Hebrews 5:12, the word translated "ought" is a word of moral or legal obligation (see Hebrews 5:3) and is often translated with reference to debt (see "owe" in Luke 16:5, 7). How would a credit card company respond if when they called to collect a monthly payment you said to them, "Yeah, I really ought to pay that. Maybe next month." If this was your response month after month, they would exercise their right to take legal action against you. And so it is with God. He says in 5:12 that they ought to be teachers and goes on to command them in Hebrews 6:1 to press on to maturity. He gives a warning that if His demand for growth is continually met with complacency, there will be dire consequences, including cursing and burning. Essentially, failure to grow doesn't just lead to falling away; failure to grow is falling away.

Take a moment to absorb that thought and reflect on your own spiritual life. Are you growing? Where are you now as compared to a year ago? Are you stronger? More able to resist temptation? Bolder in proclaiming the faith? Less anxious and more trusting of God? More apt to pray than worry? If not, then you need to heed this warning!

Are you growing?

If so, pray and thank God for your growth and ask Him to continue to bless you. If not, it's time to repent. Pray and ask God to forgive you.

Whether you answered above with yes or no, growth needs to continue to happen. What area of your spiritual life needs the most work? Rank these areas 1-10, with 1 being the area that needs the most growth:

_____ Prayer
_____ Knowledge/ study
_____ Resisting temptation
_____ Sharing your faith/ evangelism
_____ Trust/ faith
_____ Ministering to/ encouraging the brethren
_____ Fulfilling your God-given role (as wife, mother, etc.)
_____ Singing praises (not technique, but as in Colossians 3:16)
_____ Giving
_____ Caring for the poor

First pray and ask God to help you grow. Remember that He gives wisdom without reproach and we are commanded to approach the throne! (James 1:5, Hebrews 4:16).

Then make a list of three specific things you can do to grow in the area you listed as number one. You may want to set yourself a deadline for accomplishing each of these three things. If you're having a hard time thinking of how you can grow, pray about that and come back to this in a few days.

Read Hebrews 5:12 and 6:1.

If we were giving out awards for best translation based solely on these two verses, the New Revised Standard would win and the New American Standard would get a giant FAIL sign. You might recall that in discussing Hebrews 5:12 we talked about the word translated "elementary." It has to do with basic building blocks, with basic elements. Think of the periodic table of elements. While "elementary" does convey that thought, it is not the first meaning we think of when we read this word, especially when the recipients are being compared with children. Instead, we think of elementary school, the place where basics are learned. The NRSV translates that same word in Hebrews 5:12 as "basic elements." Excellent choice. Now look at Hebrews 6:1. In the New American Standard we again see "elementary," but this is an entirely different word in the Greek text. The word used here really has more of an idea of basic teaching, which is exactly how the NRSV translates it. The idea is that it is time for the recipients of this letter to move past basic teachings and move on toward more mature, "meaty" matters.

Read Hebrews 6:1, 2.

The Hebrews writer gives a list of teachings he does not want to discuss because they are simply too basic. If I want my child to grow, there comes a time when he must receive more than milk, whether he wants to or not. Likewise, with these Christians, it is time to move on. Repentance is the change of heart necessary before becoming a Christian, and also necessary when finding oneself in sin afterward (cf. Acts 2:38, Revelation 3:3). "Instructions about washings" refers to the different baptisms which needed to be distinguished in the first century (i.e. John's baptism vs. Christian baptism). Laying on of hands was likely something common in the first century. Since this is how many healings were done, people were appointed to various offices and miraculous gifts were passed on. Resurrection is listed as one of the basic points of the gospel in 1 Corinthians 15:3, 4. Eternal judgment is the very reason we came to Christ. All these things are basics likely learned early on in one's Christian life, if not before.

Read Hebrews 6:3.

The Hebrews writer seems to acknowledge God in the writing process here.

Read 2 Peter 1:20, 21.

What correlation do you see between these verses and Hebrews 6:3?

Read Hebrews 6:4-6.

The Hebrews writer lists five blessings one experiences as a Christian. Complete the list:

1. Been enlightened
2. _____
3. _____
4. _____
5. _____

"Tasted" is not like when you went the ice cream shop and they gave you a tiny spoonful. It's more like how we treat the hot, buttery rolls at a great steak place. "'Taste' is more literally 'eat' and figuratively here, 'to experience to the full extent' (see [Hebrews] 2:9)."[6] This is the same word in Hebrews 6:5 ("tasted the good word...").

"Partakers" refers to people who have shared together in something (see Hebrews 3:1, 14).

God has given good gifts— the very best He has—in hopes of enticing mankind to follow faithfully. If those who have been partakers of and have experienced fully His gifts, then turn their backs on these gifts, what else can He give? It is then impossible to renew them. Why? Because they are continually crucifying the Son of God and continually putting Him to shame. The majority of our most reliable translations do not do justice to Hebrews 6:6. The NRSV, though, shines: "and then have fallen away, since on their own they are crucifying again the Son of God and are holding him up to contempt." "Crucifying" and "holding up to contempt" are continual actions in the Greek. One who falls away is impossible to renew because they are still in the act of humiliating the very gift sent to save them. Should they choose to return to a life of repentance on their own, they are able to renew themselves, but God will not force them, and we cannot convince them. There is nothing left to give or to offer.

SIDE STUDY:

Many denominations teach that it is impossible to lose your salvation (often referred to as "once saved, always saved"). It is a commonly held belief among those who call themselves Christians that if one does appear to fall away, it is only evidence that they were never truly converted. They quote 1 John 2:19 and say that the very fact that the lost person has left our fellowship is proof that sincerity was always lacking. However, everything the Hebrews writer says in Hebrew 6:4-6 seems to point to a truly converted, God-acknowledged Christian. How do we reconcile these passages?

First, we read them in context. We have already been studying Hebrews 6 in context, so read 1 John 2:18-26.

Who is it that "went out from us"?
According to this passage, who is the antichrist?
According to 1 John 2:26, who was John writing about?

When we put the pieces together, we see that John is writing about people who purposely set out to deceive the brethren, people who denied Jesus as the Christ, and lied. They were truly never part of the fellowship; they were essentially wolves in sheep's clothing.

Is the kind of person John mentions the same kind of person as the Hebrews writer in Hebrews 6?

When we examine the contexts, we can see that these two passages are not in conflict at all. Those of whom John speaks never had salvation to begin with. They went out of fellowship with the brethren because they were never truly in fellowship with them. 1 John 2:20 says, "But you have an anointing from the Holy One..." This statement is in contrast to those who left. We then infer that those who left do not have the anointing.

But were those of Hebrews 6 really different from those of 1 John 2? Yes. Read Hebrews 6:4 again and then read Acts 2:38; Ephesians 1:13, 14; and 2 Corinthians 5:5.

In Acts, we read that the Holy Spirit is given after sins are forgiven. In Ephesians, we read that the Holy Spirit seals us in God. 2 Corinthians tells us that the Spirit is given as a pledge— as a down payment, in essence. Those the Hebrews writer talks about in Hebrews 6:4 were partakers of the Holy Spirit. They had their sins forgiven, they had been sealed in God, and had His pledge of eternal life. I don't know about you, but to me that sounds like someone who is really and truly a Christian not only in the eyes of man, but in the eyes of God!

But they have fallen away, and in their falling away, it is as though they are crucifying the Son of God, holding Him up to contempt and shame again, and again, and again, and again...

So there is nothing left for God to give. You and I cannot renew them to repentance; they already know better than to act as they are. They must decide on their own to return. What is said of addicts is true of the fallen away brother or sister: you can't help someone who doesn't want to be helped.

Read Hebrews 6:7-8.

The ground is given rain and, in a sense, has two choices of what it will do with that rain. If it produces something useful, the ground is blessed. If, on the other hand, it produces plants which are a scourge, it proves itself useless and ends up being burned. The illustration serves as a warning to the reader, and it ought to serve as a warning to us. If you have obeyed the gospel and been sealed with the Holy Spirit at baptism, then you have been given the very best of God's manifold gifts and ought to produce fruit with it, including spiritual growth in your own life.

Read Hebrews 6:9.

Were you getting scared for the recipients of this exhortation? I was! Maybe they were too, so here the writer assures them that he expects a better end for them, even though he is giving them this stern warning.

Read Hebrews 6:10-12.

In verse 10, how were the recipients said to have shown love toward God's name?

Hebrews 6:11 charges the readers to apply the same diligence they had been showing in ministering to other areas so that they will not become sluggish. The word for "diligence" is translated in 2 Timothy 4:9, 21 as "make every effort." This is a word which means to do your best, to be eager. The word translated "sluggish" was in Hebrews 5:11 and translated as "dull" of hearing. Here the author offers a solution for their dull hearing, and, as is often the case, the solution is to do the opposite (see Ephesians 4:28). If they apply the diligence they are already familiar with to more areas, they will gain full assurance of hope, cure their sluggishness, and make them imitators of the great forerunners of the faith who inherited their own promises.

Patience, endurance, etc. are key thoughts in the book of Hebrews. If you're a Bible marker, pick a color to use for this concept. It's going to come up again!

Read Hebrews 6:13-16.

Abraham received God's promise and waited with faith and patience (cf. Hebrews 6:12). His patience paid off when he received the promise, and the Hebrews' patience will pay off when they receive the promise— the "things that accompany salvation" (Hebrews 6:9).

Men today, in giving another assurance of their promise, may swear by something greater than themselves. They may swear "on

Momma's grave" or "to God" or "on a stack of Bibles," but God has only Himself to swear by. God, in giving both an oath and swearing by Himself gave Abraham the strongest possible assurance (cf. Genesis 22:16).

Hebrews 6:15 claims that Abraham obtained the promise, but Hebrews 11:13 and 39 both claim that our forerunners did not obtain the promises. Recall, though, that Abraham's promise was more than just a son. He was also promised that all nations would be blessed through Him. This was only realized in Christ. In this way, the full promise was not received even though part was.

Read Hebrews 6:17-18.

"Heirs of the promise" is us! God desired even more to show us that He would maintain His focus on fulfilling the promises. Here we have subtle praise for the written word. Why did God swear by Himself? It was not solely for Abraham's benefit, but also for Moses who would later write this account, and for those of us who would later read the account. "Interpose" is actually a word meaning a "mediator." In a sense, God's oath acted like a co-signer to guarantee His promise. Thus, we have both the promise and His confirming oath to show us God's purpose in saving us. Because of this, we have "strong encouragement" to take hold of the hope God has set before us, that is, the assurance of salvation and eternal life. "Encouragement" is also translated "exhortation" in Hebrews 12:5— this is more than simply saying "you might want to take hold of that hope there." "Take hold" is the same word as we found in Hebrews 3:14 (see study on chapter three for a full discussion).

Read Hebrews 6:19-20.

What strong imagery this is! The anchor on a ship is a vital piece. When the ship is stopped, the boat must not drift away, so the anchor is dropped. If a ship needs to keep its place in a violent storm, the anchor is dropped. The anchor is what holds the boat where it needs to be, keeping her passengers from being lost.

Likewise, the hope that God has laid before us anchors our very soul. It is as though when we became Christians, we threw our anchor to Christ, who is on the other side, where we long to be, and He holds it there for us, anchoring the only thing that matters to the only place that will last, except eternal fire. In the movies, sometimes the anchor of the ship is cut lose in the most desperate of circumstances. It is often the signal that those on the boat are surely doomed. Of course, in the movies there is usually a happy ending and the crew survives despite such dire circumstances, which causes rejoicing in the end. For us, though, there is no happy ending if we cut anchor. We have been warned and even scolded through the chapter, but we have also been given great assurance that our God, who is higher than all, will never change His purpose in granting us rest and eternal life. "We have an anchor to keep our souls, steadfast and sure, while the billows (of life) roll." We must take hold and hold fast, because Jesus is there. He has shown the way and keeps our place there beyond the veil.

Chapter 6
God's Appointed Priest

A bit of a confession is in order. Each lesson so far has advised you to read the entire book in one sitting. Sometimes that is an overwhelming task. Sure, it's supposed to only take 26 minutes, but if you're like me, finding 26 quiet minutes all in a row during a time of day when your brain is still functional might just feel impossible. Study on anyway. It would be ideal for you to read through the book in one sitting and then focus in on a chapter, but if you can't seem to make it happen, just jump in. You may want to consider listening to an audio version (there are many available for free online) while doing the dishes, driving, or whatever. Even if it is on in the background, it may be helpful to your study. With that said, if/when you read through the book this week, watch for (and mark, if you're a Bible marker) references to priests, the priesthood, etc.

After an interlude of warning and encouragement, the Hebrews writer again returns to the subject of Melchizedek. This Mel guy was a huge fascination to the Jews and has been to many scholars for some time. Theories as to his identity abound, but this is not the Hebrews writer's point. In fact, let's skip ahead a bit and see just what his point is. Hebrews 8:1 tells us exactly what the point is: we have a priest who is just such a priest and king as Melchizedek. He sits at the right hand of the throne, and He ministers in the true tabernacle made by God, not by men.

Hebrews 7 is kind of a notoriously confusing chapter, but if we keep the main point in mind, it'll be easier. Honestly, sometimes when I am having a hard time understanding a portion of scripture, I find it's best to ask myself "Do I get the gist of it? Am I getting caught up in the details?" If I do understand the gist of it, I usually call it good study for the time being. After the main point has a chance to sink it, I can come back and better understand the details. Sometimes we just have to allow ourselves some time to let things sink in, and maybe even allow ourselves to mature. I say all that to say this: if you're confused, it's okay. It's okay to not understand everything right now, but don't give up. Press on, and eventually you'll get it, even if you have to walk away from a particular passage for a bit.

Read Hebrews 7:1-2.

Melchizedek is only found in two Old Testament passages: Genesis 14:18-20 and Psalm 110:4. It is only here, in the book of Hebrews, where we discover his significance. Perhaps this is some of what the prophets and angels were longing to look into (1 Peter 1:10-12). First the author reminds his readers of who he's talking about and some of the pertinent details.

We are so very blessed to live in the time that we live in! We, as those living in the last age, have the privilege of seeing God's mysteries revealed. We have His word to guide us and here in

America, many of us have multiple copies of His word. We have Bibles on our phones, in our purses, everywhere. It can become so commonplace to us that we forget there are those, especially in other countries, who are still longing to look into these things, just as the angels.

Take a moment to pray for those who have no Bibles and those who have not been exposed to God's word, both here and abroad. If you are in a group, discuss how you can help others. List out a few ways you can help.

Read Hebrews 7:3.

One of the most interesting pieces of the Melchizedek puzzle is that we have no idea where he came from. There is no genealogy recorded, neither his birth nor his death are recorded. For all intents and purposes, he's still a priest (cf. Psalm 110:4). More importantly, his lack of genealogy combined with the fact that he pre-dates Levi and Aaron means his priesthood was not based on lineage. In the Jewish system of the Hebrews writer's day, one who could not prove their lineage could not serve as a priest. So how did Melchizedek serve? By divine appointment, the same as Jesus.

Read Hebrews 7:4-10.

Abraham was the nation's patriarch, and, to the Jews, there was no greater man. Yet here we have Abraham paying tithes to and being blessed by this out-of-nowhere priest and king. Both of these happenings show Melchizedek to be greater than Abraham, and by extension, greater than Levi and the Levitical priesthood.

If he is greater and Jesus is a priest in his order, then Christ and His ministry as priest are also greater. If you recall, this is the main point of the book of Hebrews: to prove the superiority of Christ and Christianity to Judaism.

Complete the chart of points proving Melchizedek's greatness:

Melchizedek		Abraham/ Levi	
Received tithes	(Heb. 7:6)		(Heb. 7:4)
Gave a blessing	(Heb. 7:6)		(Heb. 7:6)
	(Heb. 7:8)	Mortal	(Heb. 7:8)
	(Heb. 7:6)	Genealogy through Levi only	(Heb. 7:5)

In Hebrews 7:7, the writer mentions that the lesser (Abraham, in this case) is blessed by the greater (Melchizedek, in this case). "Greater" (superior/ better) is found 13 times in the book of Hebrews with reference to things pertaining to the new covenant versus things pertaining to the old covenant (including life before Christ and after). Bible markers may be interested to mark these instances: Hebrews 1:4; 6:9; 7:7, 19, 22; 8:6 (2x); 9:23; 10:34; 11:16, 35, 40; 12:24.

Read Hebrews 7:11-12.

Here the Hebrews writer kind of says, "If it wasn't broken, it wouldn't have needed to be fixed." But it wasn't broken, exactly, it just wasn't God's final goal. It was a stepping stone, and the Jewish Christians needed to understand that. (Note: "Perfection" [perfect, perfected, made perfect] is another key word in the book of Hebrews.

Bible markers, here's a list of the occurrences: Hebrews 2:10; 5:9, 14; 6:1; 7:11, 19, 28; 9:9, 11; 10:1, 14; 11:40; 12:23.)

Something else the Jews needed to understand is that since the priesthood and the law are inextricably linked, a change of one necessitates the change of the other.

Read Hebrews 7:13-14.

"For the one concerning whom these things are spoken" must refer to Jesus since there were no tribes during Melchizedek's time. Jesus was of the tribe of Judah and since there were no priests from the tribe of Judah, He could not have been a Levitical priest. The Hebrews writer makes an argument here from the silence of scripture. In Exodus 28-29 and Leviticus 8-9, God makes plain the requirements of those serving in the priesthood. Among those requirements are that the officiant must be of the line of Aaron (Exodus 28:1, 41). Having said what He does want (priests from the sons of Aaron), He does not have to specify what He does not want (priests from any other tribe or line). This is relevant to us today as a hermeneutical (remember, hermeneutics tells us how to study our Bible) principle. If God specifies what He wants in a particular area, we would be sinfully going against Him to add on to it, just as the Jews would have been sinning to name a priest from any tribe but Levi.

Read Hebrews 7:15-17.

Christ became a priest based on something far more substantial than his parentage. He became a priest based on immortality! This verse goes back to verse 11. The word for "another" here is HETEROS— another of a different kind. Jesus became a priest of a different kind than the Levitical priests and the requirements of this priesthood are such that no Levite could match up.

What requirements (discussed here) are there for each kind of priesthood?

Levitical:

Melchizedekian:

Read Hebrews 7:18-19

Fill in this chart:

Old Law/Priesthood		New Covenant/Priesthood	
1)	(Heb. 7:18)	1)	(Heb. 7:19)
2)	(Heb. 7:18)	2)	(Heb. 7:19)
3)	(Heb. 7:19)		

Bible markers: Check out these occurrences of the phrase "draw near" or "come" (from ENGIZO and PROSERCHOMAI) and decide if it is a phrase you want to mark: Hebrews 4:16; 7:19, 25; 10:1, 22, 25; 11:6; 12:18, 22.

Read Hebrews 7:20-22.

Here we have the second oath concerning the new covenant. God swore by Himself (because there was none greater to swear by) to Abraham concerning the promises given him (Hebrews 7:13), and here God gives an oath that the Christ will be a priest forever.

The old law, in contrast, has no oaths for priests, and God gave no oaths concerning them. Score another point for the new, better covenant. Furthermore, Jesus is God's guarantee, His promise and seal that this IS a better covenant. They need not fear moving on from what they are familiar with, what their fore-bearers handed down to them because God has given a guarantee— Jesus— that this new way is a better way.

Read Hebrews 7:23-25.

Every Levitical priest had one major flaw: they were prevented from service by death. "Thus by its very set up the old priesthood was unstable and inferior. Josephus records that there were a total of 83 High Priests from Aaron to the destruction of the temple in 70 AD (Antiquities 20.227). Jesus comes into priesthood with 'an indestructible life' (v. 16) and an oath saying that He would abide forever as a priest (cf. v. 21)"[7] Since Jesus lives on, He is always there for us, always able to save us, help us to draw near and offer intercession for us. Intercession means "to make an earnest request through contact with the person approached."[8] We have a High Priest who lives forever, seated at the right hand of the throne of God who is perpetually making an earnest request with God Himself on our behalf! THAT is awesome.

Read Hebrews 7:26.

"Fitting" seems an odd word here. It seems to say that we deserved this kind of High Priest, but that isn't what is meant at all. This is the same word we find in Hebrews 2:10 describing why the Christ had to suffer. It was what was proper to get the job done right. Likewise, to properly save His dear creation, it was proper that God put such a High Priest as Jesus in place.

Use Strong's Concordance or BlueLetterBible.org to fine the meaning of the undefined words below.

This High Priest is...

- holy— undefiled by sin, free from wickedness, religiously observing every moral obligation, pure holy, pious
- innocent (harmless, KJV)—
- undefiled—
- separated from sinners— apart from those devoted to sin
- exalted above the heavens— high, lifted up; eminent, exalted above the expanse of the sky

Read Hebrews 7:27-28.

We have in Hebrews 7:26-28 a summation of sorts of the entire chapter. Not only is Jesus all those things we find in verse 26, but He, in His sinlessness does not need to offer a sacrifice for His own sins. He also has no need to offer sacrifices daily because He did so once when He gave His own life and body as sacrifice. Unlike those appointed under the Mosaic Law, Jesus is not weak or mortal. Rather, He is a High Priest appointed by the very oath of God to serve in His perfection forever.

Chapter 7

New and Improved

This week as you read through the book of Hebrews in one sitting, watch for the word "covenant" and notice its significance. Bible markers, this is definitely a key word and should be marked. In the NASB there are 21 occurrences.

Read Hebrews 8:1-3.

This statement sums up chapter seven as well as the author's main point since Hebrews 4:14. He has painted a picture of just who Jesus is as High Priest.

"Such" refers to something that fits the description given. Jesus is exactly the kind of High Priest that's been discussed to this point, as amazing as that is. He is a minister in the true tabernacle, that is, not the copy (as earthly priests were serving in) but the original, heavenly tabernacle pitched by God Himself. Obviously, this tabernacle would be superior to the one found on earth in Jerusalem. Not only is the tabernacle superior, but the offering is as well since Christ offers Himself.

Read Hebrews 8:4.

Jesus could not be a priest on earth, not only because He is descended from Judah (Hebrews 7:14), but also because the position is filled. As a side note, verses such as this one indicate the book of Hebrews was written prior to AD 70 when the temple at Jerusalem was destroyed. Bible markers may want to mark this verse in some way. Personally, when I come across verses which reference time or indicate a date, I draw a green clock in the margin. If you are reading a commentary or some other extra-biblical source, knowing true dates of Bible books can be especially useful. Sources that are less-than-sound will often show their hand in their dating of books.

Read Hebrews 8:5.

The original readers of Hebrews were apparently considering leaving their Christian faith and going back to their Jewish ways. They needed to realize that worship in the temple was but a shadow, a mere reflection of the true worship God had always had in Heaven itself. Why was Moses warned so sternly to make the tabernacle to such specific standards? Because he was creating an earthly version of the true, heavenly tabernacle.

We have things in our lives today which are a shadow of Heaven. Christian fellowship, the genuine love between friends, and other such things. Take a moment to dream! Dwell on what glories await in Heaven by considering those things which are a shadow of what is to come and list a few here.

Read Hebrews 8:6-7.

This is a key statement of the book (note to Bible markers: you may want to mark this key statement in some way. I draw a key in the margin). It is a summation of several arguments, giving four reasons (three positive, one negative) as to why what we have through Christ is better. List them here:

_____

_____

_____

_____

_____

"Excellent" is the same word as 1:4 regarding the more excellent name Jesus has. Something excellent is different with a focus on value. It's outstanding because of its quality. In this case, Jesus' ministry is outstanding because He is the mediator of a better covenant, which is based on better promises and replaces a faulty covenant.

But wait a minute… God is the one who made the first covenant. How could it be less than perfect or faultless? Here are two possibilities offered by Denny Petrillo in his notes given to the Workshop in the Word attendees in 1999.

1. God designed it so that it would be seen to fall far short of the beauty and effectiveness of the New Covenant.

2. Men, through their own sinful choices, failed to live up to the high level of spirituality designed by the old covenant.

Read Hebrews 8:8, 9.

Here the writer quotes from Jeremiah 31:31-34 and foretells the coming of a new covenant. The gospels talk of the redemptive work of Christ, which forms the basis for making the new covenant possible (it is not in itself part of the new covenant). When the gospel was preached in Acts 2, the new covenant was offered to people. Each time an individual person accepts God's offer to enter into a covenant by being baptized into Christ, there is a covenant between God and that person (Galatians 3:27). The terms of this covenant are found in the Scriptures. The agreement itself is between God and each person.

He says this new covenant will not be like the one He had before. Without question, Jeremiah (and the Hebrews writer) are speaking of the covenant made with Israel in the wilderness at Mount Sinai, of which Moses was the mediator. There are those who hold to the Old Testament (note that "testament" is a synonym of "covenant") still today and want to bind portions of it, but God through two prophets expressly says He will give a new covenant to replace the faulty one. There can be no doubt that God has a new contract/ covenant/ testament with mankind. Just as old real estate contracts or employment contracts, or any number of various contracts would be kept as reference and would offer insight as well as information, so it is with the Old Testament today. We learn valuable lessons from God's dealings with the Israelites, but it is not binding on us today. If we want to be in a relationship with God, we must access Him through the prescribed method of the New Testament: immersion for the forgiveness of sins into Christ (Acts 2:38; Galatians 3:27).

Depending on what version you are reading, the end of Hebrews 8:9 can be confusing. The NASB reads "…and I did not care for them, says the Lord." The way we use this phrase today means something entirely different than what is meant here. If I say I didn't care for the spinach casserole, it means I didn't like it at all. This is more literal, though. The word here means that God did not take care of them. They, like the nations around them, had chosen to go their own way and God allowed them to do just that (cf. Romans 1:28). In Deuteronomy 28:15-68, God outlines what will befall the people of Israel should they choose to disobey the Lord and not continue in God's covenant. They chose not to continue and thus God did as He said He would. The fault of the covenant was the Israelites themselves. If I start a diet plan and spend more time "cheating" than following the diet, where does the fault lie: with the diet or with me? Of course, the fault lies with me, just as the fault of God's covenant was with the Israelites.

Though the covenant spoken of here is new, there are similarities as well. The primary similarity is the origin of the covenant. Three times from Hebrews 8:8-10 we are told who the maker of the covenants is.

Complete the chart:

Verse	God says ...
(Heb 8:8)	
	... which I made ...
(Heb. 8:10)	

Note what Petrillo writes: "...the new [covenant], like the old, was a unilateral covenant. That means that it originated from God and from Him alone... Since it is a unilateral covenant, man is in no position to change, alter or neglect any of the stipulations of the covenant/ contract."[9]

Read Hebrews 8:10-12.

God goes on to describe more of His new covenant. The people will be educated concerning His laws. Note that these are His laws and that, yes, there are laws in this new covenant. There are those who say the New Testament is simply a love letter from God and there is no pattern or law to be obeyed. God clearly disagrees. In fact, so important are these laws that He wants them written on the hearts of His people.

Read Psalm 1:1-3.

This is a description of one for whom the Law is in his heart. There are things he does, and things he does not do. Fill in the verses:

He does ...	He does not ...	Because of this ...
delight in the law of the Lord ____:____	walk in the counsel of the wicked ____:____	he is like a tree firmly planted by streams of water ____:____
meditate in the law day and night ____:____	stand in the path of sinners ____:____	yields fruit in season ____:____
	sit in the seat of scoffers ____:____	leaf does not wither ____:____
		whatever he does prospers ____:____

In the Old Testament, one entered into a covenant relationship with God from infancy. A boy was circumcised on the eighth day, which entered him into covenant with God; he would need to be taught throughout his life who God is, etc. The new covenant is different, though. One must know of God and (at least some of) His ways before joining His covenant (cf. Matthew 28:19). This relationship is one we must choose for ourselves (note: consider what impact this has on the false doctrine of infant baptism).

The reward for being in this relationship with God is abundant: He is merciful to us and remembers our sins no more. Because God is omniscient, it cannot be that He literally does not remember our sins. Rather, He chooses not to act on them. When Noah was in the ark, the account says "God remembered Noah…" (Genesis 8:1). Are we to believe that God had forgotten of Noah's existence or failed to notice the situation? Of course not. But it is at this point when God took action on the ark-dwellers' behalf. With our sins, it is the opposite. God remembers our sins no more. He chooses not to act on them.

Read Hebrews 8:13.

"Obsolete" means to become old or to wear out. It's a word that may not be in most everyday conversations, but it's a concept we're familiar with. Remember car phones? They are obsolete today. How about records, eight tracks, cassette tapes, VHS tapes and VHS players? Each of them is obsolete. They've all been replaced by something new and better. So it is with the old law. Would you really like to go back to a car phone or a bag phone? I am certainly glad that, aside from camping, outhouses are obsolete in America. I don't yearn for those days (or at least not that particular aspect!). Likewise, the readers of this exhortation need to get with the times and adopt the new covenant God has so painstakingly laid out.

Chapter 8

A Way Into The Holy Place

As you read this week, notice how many times the word "tabernacle" is used (you'll find it's primarily in chapter nine), and pay attention to the "pilgrimage" message— that our stay here is temporary, that we are seeking eternal rest.

Read Hebrews 9:1-5.

Hebrews 9:1 refers to the "earthly sanctuary," as opposed to the Heavenly sanctuary in the true tabernacle pitched by God Himself in the heavens (Hebrews 8:1, 2).

Hebrews 9:2 begins a discussion of the tabernacle and its layout. The tabernacle... not the temple. Why is that? The tabernacle is that which was given to Moses as an earthly model of what is in the heavenly realms.

What was contained in the ark of the covenant? (Hebrews 9:4).

What was on top of the ark of the covenant?
(Hebrews 9:5).

We run into some confusion when we read Hebrews 9:4 and compare it with Exodus 30:1-6. Exodus 30:6 places the altar of incense outside the Holy of Holies in the Holy Place, but Hebrews 9:4 seems to place it inside. So, which is it? Both. Kind of. The altar of incense itself was to be placed in front of the veil inside the Holy Place, and the smoke of the incense was to flow into the Holy of Holies, covering the "stench" of sin. Additionally, some scholars have noted that the wording of Hebrews 9:3-4 "allows for the altar reference to mean that it 'pertains' to the Holy of Holies'"[10]

Read Hebrews 9:6-7.

Earthly priests entered the holy place (or the outer tabernacle) daily to keep the altar of incense burning and fulfill their other duties. Only the High Priest could enter the Holy of Holies, though. Even still, he could only go in once a year on the Day of Atonement, and only after going through all the prescribed rituals (see Leviticus 16). He entered once that day to offer blood for his own sins and once for the since of the people. It's such a contrast compared to the privileges we have that it bears some meditation. We are so accustomed to having constant and free access to God that we take it for granted.

In the tabernacle, there was the courtyard, the outer tabernacle (Holy Place) and the Holy of Holies. Where did

God (representatively) dwell?

Who, then, had access to God and how often? (cf. Hebrews 9:7).

Read Hebrews 9:8-10.

So long as the tabernacle (and the temple, which was really just a more solid tabernacle as far as religious significance) was standing and in use by God's people, the way to the true holy place could not be disclosed (revealed, exposed publicly). The "outer tabernacle" represents the whole structure. Literally, this is the "first" tabernacle; there may be a footnote indicating this in your Bible.

The Hebrews writer says the tabernacle is a symbol for this time. The word for "symbol" is PARABOLE. Look familiar? Jesus spoke many things in PARABOLAIS (Matthew 13:3). The tabernacle, then, is an earthly thing with a heavenly significance.

Read Hebrews 10:19-20.

What is the way into the Holy Place?

(Bible markers may want to underline "the way into the holy place" in Hebrews 9:8 and write "cf. Hebrews 10:19-20" in the margin. In Hebrews 10:19-20, underline "enter the holy place" and "new and living way." Note: "cf." stands for "cross reference.")

Just as the tabernacle could never reveal the true way to the holy place as long as it was in service, so it was with the sacrifices. They had only to do with the body, not with one's conscience. "Perfect" here is TELIOO (see Lesson 5, notes on Hebrews 5:9-10). These sacrifices couldn't complete the worshiper, so they were only meant to remain in place until a time of reformation. The reformation is the new covenant which we now live under. It was ushered in when Christ appeared as a high priest (Hebrews 9:11).

Read Hebrews 9:11-14.

Here the Hebrews writer really shifts into high gear and begins explaining how all the tabernacle and sacrifice talk relates to the readers. He explains how the new covenant is better than the old in these regards, as well as those already discussed.

"Good things to come" refers to those things which were foreshadowed: To everything that the earthly sanctuary (Hebrews 9:1) and its sacrifices pointed to in the heavens and in Jesus' service. His entrance into the tabernacle (which itself was greater and more perfect/ complete) was not via an animal's blood, but rather, it was by His own, freely given blood.

Consider this from Guy Orbison:[11]

"Which would help you most?

1. A priest who could only enter an earthly tabernacle or a priest who entered into heaven?
2. The sacrificial blood of animals or the blood of a blameless being who made the decision to die FOR you?

Since we have the greater...

1. ...our conscience can be actually cleansed.
2. ...it should move us from 'dead works' to truly serve God."

Read Hebrews 9:15-17.

"For this reason"— Via this new way, through this greater, more perfect tabernacle, we can actually have our consciences cleansed, and because of this, Jesus became the mediator of a new covenant. It was not for His own benefit the new covenant was inaugurated. It was for our benefit and for the people of the old covenant. His sacrifice covered the sins of all people, of all nations, of all time.

Both the old and new testaments/ covenants are similar to a Last Will and Testament in that they require a death to go into effect. If your grandfather's will leaves you $10,000,000 it does not mean much until he actually passes away. Up to that point, it is only a promise, not an actual covenant or testament. So it was with this new, better covenant. A death was required, and Jesus provided that for us.

Read Hebrews 9:18-22.

Here the Hebrews writer references the beginning of God's covenant with the Israelite nation.

Read Exodus 24:3-8. What differences do you see between this passage and what we just read in Hebrews?

These differences can be accounted for in a couple of ways. The most obvious answer is that the Hebrews writer adds previously unknown details through inspiration of the Holy Spirit. Also, consider that hyssop and scarlet wool were common in other cleanings (cf. Leviticus 14:1-9, Numbers 19:1-10).

Read Hebrews 9:23-26.

The blood of young bulls and goats was sufficient for the earthly sanctuary, a mere copy, but the real thing required better sacrifices, especially since its cleansing and sacrifice was a one-time-only occurrence. In the earthly tabernacle, God dwelt representatively in the Holy of Holies, but in the true tabernacle, Christ appeared in the actual presence of God. The earthly high priest comes year after year to offer sacrifice for sins, but Christ's sacrifice was such that it only needed to be offered once. He offered His sacrifice at the "consummation of the ages." The word translated "consummation" is another word rooted in TELIOS. It was the complete or perfect time for the new covenant to begin, the fulfillment of God's ultimate plan. By this sacrifice, sins were put away. "Put away" means to render something void. If I have a coupon for buy one, get one free, it may have something like "Void after January 31, 2012" on it. If I take that to the store today, they won't honor it because it isn't valid any more. At one time, the accuser had something on us. He had a "certificate of debt" and we were dead in our transgressions (Colossians 2:13, 14). Now, though, thanks to the sacrifice of Christ, that certificate has been voided. It has been put away, it won't be honored by God, and we will not have to pay the price for it.

SIDE STUDY
Read Hebrews 7:18.
The same word used in Hebrews 9:26 to express what has happened with our sins is also used in Hebrews 7:18 to express what has happened with the old covenant. Just as the old covenant

was set aside, so our sins are set aside. There are some parallels we can draw. We learn from the old covenant about the nature of God, but we do not follow it. Likewise, we can learn from our old, sinful ways about our own nature as well as use those experiences to minister to others, but we do not follow those ways any longer.

The usage of this word also provides an illustration for our friends in the Seventh Day Adventist faith, and others who may want to retain portions of the Old Testament as binding today. The old covenant is just as "set aside" or "put away" as our sins are. If the old covenant is only partially put away, then we must say the same of our sins. I don't know about you, but that's not a particularly appealing thought to me!

Complete the chart below.

	Earthly tabernacle	Heavenly tabernacle
sacrifice(s) accomplishes…	cleansing of the flesh (Heb. 9:13)	(Heb. 9:14)
cleansed with…	blood of animals (Heb. 9:19)	(Heb. 9:23)
sacrifice offered…	(Heb. 9:19)	once (Heb. 9:12, 26)
holy place…	made with hands	(Heb. 9:24)

Read Hebrews 9:27-28.

You only live once, and you only die once, and then you go to judgment. Likewise, Christ died once (as sacrifice for our sins), and when he comes again, it will be to impart salvation to those who are eagerly awaiting him. A child who knows that the ice cream truck comes by at 3:15 every afternoon may stand at the door, dollar in hand, at 3:00. He is ready and anxious, yet patient. This is how the

Christian waits for Christ to come a second time. We are ready. We are anxious for our new home. But we are patient, knowing that the patience of God means the salvation of many (2 Peter 3:9).

Chapter 9

Inside the Inner Circle

In this chapter, we are rapidly ascending the mountain of evidence which proves the superiority of the new, better covenant, and we are about to reach the very pinnacle. This chapter will be divided into two lessons in order to give adequate attention to that pinnacle. The Hebrews writer was truly a master craftsman, and here he ties up loose ends, drawing the reader to the inescapable conclusion that there can be nothing better than what we have been given.

Read Hebrews 10:1-2.

Below you will find these verses quoted and the portions to be discussed underlined.

"For the Law, since it has only a shadow of the good things to come and not the very form of things, can never, by the same sacrifices which they offer continually year by year, make perfect those who draw near. Otherwise, would they not have ceased to be offered, because the worshipers, having once been cleansed, would no longer have had consciousness of sins? But in those sacrifices there is reminder of sins year by year. For it is impossible for the blood of bulls and goats to take away sins."

Only a shadow— The idea of the Jewish system as a shadow of the Heavenly reality goes back to the discussion begun in Hebrews 8:1 (8:5 especially). The Law, the priests' ministry, and the tabernacle (as well as the subsequent temple) were all simply shadows of what God had planned for His people (cf. Hebrews 9:11, 23). As such, the results were also only a shadow of the blessings. The writer has been arguing since Hebrews 9:23 that a better sacrifice was needed for the true tabernacle, and here he explains why the sacrifices of the Mosaic system were inferior: they needed to be offered continually.

Good things to come— cf. Hebrews 9:11— This refers to forgiveness as a theological reality as well as in the heart of the worshipper

Continually year by year— cf. Hebrews 9:25— likely refers to the Day of Atonement. This was an annual festival of the old covenant in which faithful Jews were required to go to Jerusalem and were to "afflict themselves," that is, to fast (Leviticus 16:29). The high priest would make a sacrifice and enter into the Holy of Holies to sprinkle blood there. This festival was, in essence, a yearly reminder of sins.

Make perfect— make complete, whole. When we are racked with guilt, it is difficult to feel whole, especially with regard to a relationship where the wrong may have occurred. Under the Mosaic system, the Jews could not draw near in the same way that we can: with confidence (Hebrews 4:16) and full assurance (Hebrews 10:22). The sacrifices could not fully heal this relationship because the blood of bulls and goats is insufficient to the task (and is even a reminder of those sins).

Bible markers: the idea of perfection in Hebrews is definitely one to mark (these are the "TEL" words we've often discussed in our notes, especially those on Hebrews 5:9-10). There are 14 occurrences: Hebrews 2:10; 6:9, 14; 6:1; 7:11, 19, 28; 9:9, 11; 10:1, 14; 11:40; 12:2, 23.

Draw near— If we boil this passage down to its bare bones, we have this: "For the Law... can never... make perfect those who draw near." Throughout the book of Hebrews, the English phrase "draw near" occurs six times. There are two Greek words used (PROSERCHOMAI and ENGIZO) and if we add the times those words are used but translated differently, we find the phrase nine times in the original language.

Fill in this chart...

Verse	drawing near through/under Christ	drawing near through/under Old Law	drawing near, misc.
Hebrews 4:16	with confidence, to throne of grace		
Hebrews 7:19 (ENGIZO)			
Hebrews 7:25	to God through Jesus		
Hebrews 10:1			
Hebrews 10:22			
Hebrews 10:25 (ENGIZO)			encourage as you see the day drawing near
Hebrews 11:6 (comes)	to God, must believe. Could be old or new law	to God, must believe. Could be old or new law	
Hebrews 12:18 (come)		to mountain— Mt. Sinai	
Hebrews 12:22 (come)	to Mount Zion, city of the living God		

After filling in this chart, Bible markers may or may not want to mark these passages.

Would they not have ceased to be offered—The very fact that the sacrifices had to be repeated speaks of their inadequacy. Martel Pace expressed this idea well in the Truth for Today Commentary on Hebrews: "If medicine has to be given over and over to a patient, it is evident that the medicine has not cured him. The disease may be arrested so that it does not further harm the patient, but this is not a total cure. Once forgiven, a person may recognize the enormity of his sins, as did Paul, and yet not be overwhelmed by dread of punishment, knowing he has full forgiveness through Christ. In contrast, the Law was designed to make the worshiper continuously uneasy regarding his sin" (Martel 376).

Would no longer have had consciousness of sins? But in those sacrifices there is reminder of sins year by year— This is a confusing passage, if you ask me, but when we take these two phrases together, it helps us understand what is being said. "Consciousness" is a word that means to be aware of information about something. In 1 Corinthians 4:4, Paul says that he is conscious (aware) of nothing against himself, of no wrong he has done. His conscience does not accuse him. Under the old law, however, such could not be said. The annual Day of Atonement and required fasting was for the very purpose of reminding the worshiper of sin.

Impossible for the blood of bulls and goats to take away sins— This is "the only obvious conclusion from (1) the evidence of repetitive animal sacrifice and (2) the understanding of the Law as 'shadow.'"[12] Then what was the purpose of these sacrifices? Remember that the very purpose of the Old Law was to explain what sin is, to show mankind its sinfulness, and to impress the need for a Savior. These sacrifices played a major role in accomplishing that goal.

Read Hebrews 10:5-10.

Here the Hebrews writer quotes from Psalm 40:6-8 to sum up what we have just discussed: it was never God's final plan or His ultimate will for sacrifices to cover the sins of His people. His ultimate will was, as Hebrews 10:9 says, to take "away the first in order to establish the second." Hebrews 10:10 states the ultimate result of Christ's sacrifice: "By this will we have been sanctified through the offering of the body of Jesus Christ once for all." Just what does it mean to be sanctified? Arndt & Gingrich says it means to "include a person in the inner circle of what is holy"[13] By the sacrifice of Christ, by His blood, we have gained passage into the Holy of Holies, the throne of grace, and we are included among those things which are holy, undeserving though we are! What an amazing truth! I remember the "cool kids" at school and wanting so much to be included in their circle, to know their secrets, to be invited to their parties, and to sit with them at lunch. For me, it never happened in school, but here, in the spiritual realm— far more important than the school cafeteria— I am included in the inner circle because of the sacrifice of Jesus Christ and the cleansing His blood affords.

Read Hebrews 10:11-18.

Continuing with our school analogy, imagine the popular kids and another kid we might have uncharitably referred to as a "wannabe." She wants so badly to be in the popular clique that she'll do anything they ask. She does their math homework for them, cleans out their lockers, brings cookies— sacrifices and sacrifices to gain access. It doesn't ever fully work, though. They're not really her friends. In our analogy, this girl is like the priests. Their sacrifices simply weren't sufficient. They were only a copy of the real thing, and no amount of sacrificing could make the shadow into the substance. Christ, on the other hand, was already in the inner circle. If the leader of the popular girls "vouched" for our wannabe and told the rest of the clique that she was cool, she would be "in," no questions asked. Christ, by His sacrifice, vouched for us. He paid the way for our passage to the inner circle, so to speak. He only had to do it once and now He is waiting for that final day when all will be set to rights and His enemies will be vanquished for all eternity.

Here's another chart to help us out, this time contrasting Hebrews 10:11, 12.[14]

Complete the chart.

Old Covenant (Hebrews 10:11)	New Covenant (Hebrews 10:12)
every priest (more than one)	(one individual)
daily ministering (more than one)	offered one sacrifice (just one)
(ineffective)	one… for all time (effective)
can never take away sins (ineffective)	for sins (effective)
stands (denotes continual ministry)	(completed ministry)

Read Hebrews 10:15-18.

The Holy Spirit testifies in scripture to God's intent before it was carried out (Note how the Holy Spirit testifies: in scripture! The Holy Spirit did not testify via a warm fuzzy feeling or an "I just know" feeling or anything else so unreliable. No, the Holy Spirit testified in scripture then as well as now, despite what our denominational friends may want us to believe.).

"Testify" here is a good translation of what is happening. Just as a witness in a court case is one who testifies based on their own knowledge of the case, so too the Holy Spirit testifies. As one of the Godhead, the Holy Spirit has personal knowledge of the intent and desires of God and testifies to this in scripture.

This is now the second time each of these scriptures has been referenced. In Hebrews 8:10-12 these verses were quoted also. By here quoting only a portion of what he has already addressed, the Hebrews writer further expands on the discussion and begins to sum up what has been said.

In Hebrews 10:3, it was noted that a disadvantage of the Old Law was that there was a continual reminder of sins. It was not only in the eyes of the people, but also in God's eyes. In the new covenant, though, there is no more remembrance of sin. Once it is forgiven, it is gone. There is no annual fasting to remind us and humble us anew.

In Hebrews 10:18, the writer states what he has been building to for some time now: there is no need for the sacrifices any longer. The ultimate sacrifice has been given, the ultimate price has been paid. To give further sacrifices would be like continuing to pay your creditor after the debt has been paid. The difference here is that doing so implies the price given was not sufficient; it insults the sacrifice of Christ. In this summation, the Hebrews writer prepares for the pinnacle of the book. He has proven from several angles that the new covenant is far superior to the old, and in Hebrews 10:19-27 he will apply these truths for the readers (including us). It is such masterful writing!

Before the next lesson, see if you can outline Hebrews 10:19-27.

Chapter 10

Encouragement and Endurance

Read Hebrews 10:19-39.

Here we have the pinnacle of the book that we've been anticipating. The structure of this section is particularly masterful. First the Hebrews writer gives the basis for the command ("therefore, brethren, since…"), gives the command ("let us…"), tells the consequences of not obeying the command ("For if…") then encourages the reader that they (we) already have what is needed to obey ("But remember…")

Fill in this outline (extra paper may be needed):

I. Therefore, since…

    A. we have confidence to enter the holy place (Hebrews 10:19)

        1. by _____ (Hebrews 10:19)

        2. by a new and living way (His flesh) (Hebrews 10:20)

    B. we have _____ (Hebrews 10:19).

II. Let us…

   A. _____ (Hebrews 10:22)

   B. hold fast (Hebrews 10:23)

   C. consider (Hebrews 10:24)

III. For if we go on sinning willfully after _____, there no longer remains a sacrifice for sins.

   A. [What remains…]

      1. _____ (Hebrews 10:27)

      2. fury of a fire which will consume the adversaries (Hebrews 10:27, Isaiah 26:11)

   B. [Judgment deserved]

      1. Anyone who has set aside the Law of Moses dies without mercy on the testimony of two or three witnesses (Hebrews 10:28)

      2. [More severe punishment for rejecting the new covenant]

      3. trampled underfoot _____ (Hebrews 10:29)

      4. _____ insulted the Spirit of grace

   C. We know Him… (Hebrews 10:30)

      1. "Vengeance is Mine, I will repay."

      2. _____ terrifying thing to fall into the hands of the _____ God (Hebrews 10:31).

IV. Confidence in the Hebrews

   A. But remember the former days when, after being enlightened… (Hebrews 10:32)

      1. You endured a great conflict of sufferings

a. being made a public spectacle

1. _____ (Hebrews 10:33)

2. tribulations

b. becoming sharers with those who were so treated.

c. showed sympathy to the prisoners (Hebrews 10:34)

d. accepted _____ the seizure of your property

1. knowing that you have for yourselves a better possession

2. [knowing that you have for yourselves] a _____ [possession]

B. Your confidence has a great reward (Hebrews 10:35).

C. You have need of endurance (Hebrews 10:36).

1. receive what has been promised

2. a very little while He is coming, and will not delay (Hebrews 10:37).

3. the righteous live by faith (Hebrews 10:38)

4. _____

5. We are… (Hebrews 10:39

a. not of those who shrink back to destruction

b. of those have faith to the preserving of the soul

With an overview of the section in hand, let's dig a little deeper and see just what makes this so masterful.

Read Hebrews 10:19-21.

Here we find a summary of many of the Hebrews writer's points so far. We have pieces of so much of the book right here! Bible markers, get ready to write in your margins! You may want to mark down cross references (commonly abbreviated "cf.") to these important themes.

The writer refers to the recipients as "brethren" at several points throughout the book, notably Hebrews 2:11, 3:12. It's a term not only of fellowship, but also the relationship we share with Jesus. He also uses the term to highlight and draw attention to key points. "Confidence" is another word which pops up at key moments, and it is one of the two "we haves" of this passage which are the basis for the coming commands (cf. Hebrews 3:6; 4:16; 6:11; 10:22,35). These verses have many similarities with Hebrews 4:14-16. There we approach the throne of grace with confidence; here we confidently enter the Holy Place, both places of petition to God. The Holy Place and Jesus' entry into the true Holy Place was discussed in Hebrews 9. Hebrews 9:8 tells us that the way into the Holy Place isn't disclosed while the first is still standing, but here we see that the way has been inaugurated, dedicated for us and it is new and living. This way through the veil is through Jesus' flesh, "... bringing to mind again the body, the death, the sacrifice, etc. As earthly priests entered through veil, so must we... the death of Jesus. No one without authority dared to enter the old Holy of Holies, but we may have confidence to enter the true holy place through Jesus."[15]

The second "we have" is a great priest. So much of the Hebrews exhortation has been about establishing Jesus, His ministry, and

His priesthood as superior to that of the earthly priests serving in earthly ministries. What we have is nothing like what was part of the old covenant. Rather, "we have such a high priest, who has taken His seat at the right hand of the throne of the Majesty in the heavens, a minister in the sanctuary and in the true tabernacle, which the Lord pitched, not man" (Hebrews 8:1, 2). His tabernacle is superior, his offering superior, his calling superior. Everything about Jesus as the great High priest is superior— and we have this priest! Not only that, but we are part of the very house of God. This priest is our brother (Hebrews 2:11) and Moses—that great mediator who brought the Law down from the mountain—was but a servant in this house (Hebrews 3:5). With all these blessings, who could think of abandoning such a way as God has laid for us?! And with all this in mind, the Hebrews writer encourages and commands in Hebrews 10:22-25.

Read Hebrews 10:22-25.

Remembering that "let us" is the hortatory form of giving a command, list the three commands.

While "let us" does indicate a command, it also encourages and subtly says "we're in this together." The Hebrews writer is not one to stand on a hill far away and say, "Go and do…" Rather, he says "let us do this together."

Bible markers may want to note the three commands in some way. I have all the "let us" passages of Hebrews circled ("let us" only; not the whole passage). Some may want to simply number these commands to point out the three in a row.

The first of three commands is to draw near. With the way dedicated for us, we can (and must) draw near with sincere hearts. This word for sincere not only means genuine (as we would define sincere), but it also means to be in accordance with what is true. The hearts of those who draw near need to be truly and genuinely in accord with these facts, being fully assured of all that the new covenant entails, assured of its supremacy, and assured of its promises. All standards are not gone with the old covenant, however. We must have our hearts sprinkled clean and our bodies washed with pure water. "Sprinkled clean" draws on the imagery of the blood-sprinkling done by priests for cleansing. Martel Pace in the Hebrews volume of Truth for Today Commentary explains the application: "If our hearts condemn us, we have a barrier between us and God, However the barrier of guilt can be overcome by the mercy of God through Jesus, for God is greater than our heart and knows all things' (1 John 3:20)" (393). Pace continues and discusses bodies washed with pure water: "This mention of 'water' in verse 22 must be a reference to baptism. It is abundantly clear in the New Testament that baptism, or immersion, was performed for the remission of sins (Acts 2:38; 22:16)" (394). Just as the priests of the old covenant could not approach the Holy of Holies without proper cleansing of themselves and the instruments of worship, neither can we hope to draw near, even on this new and living way, without a clear conscience and sins forgiven in the pure waters of baptism. I make sense of it this way: our bodies are washed with water, and our sins forgiven (Acts 2:38), but no one remains sinless (see 1 John 1:8). The Christian, however, has the continual cleansing of the Son of God, thus sprinkling our hearts (1 John 1:7). With both of these, we can (and must) draw near.

The second command is to hold fast the confession of our hope. In Hebrews 3:1, Jesus was named as the High Priest of our confession, that is, of our collective faith. Hope, in a biblical sense, is far more than a fond wish. I might say I hope it rains next week, but if I live in a desert and it's the middle of summer, I don't have much actual expectation of rain. Biblical hope, though, is assured, steady, knows that its object will come to pass. It is desire combined with expectation. For the Christian, the hope we confess encompasses all that has been promised— Jesus' return, rest to come— all of it. The foundation for this hope is the one who promised and who has proven faithful time and time again. Because of this foundation, we hold fast without leaning or giving way.

The third command is connected grammatically with the second. Part of holding our confession is to consider those around us. If we ourselves are faithful, we will consider how to help others stay faithful also. We will stimulate, stir up, provoke each other toward active love and toward doing good deeds. The choice of words here is interesting. Usually we would think of stirring up as something negative. We stir up trouble. We provoke an argument. We rouse suspicion. Yet all of these words (stir up, provoke, rouse) are valid synonyms for the word translated "stimulate" by the NASB.

How does the choice of words here reflect what it is we are to be doing for one another?

The third command has two participles connected with it. Bear in mind, the participles help describe how to fulfill the command and they end in -ing. In this case, the command is to consider each other. But how do we do that? By (a) not forsaking the assembly of the saints and by (b) encouraging one another. (Note: "assembling" looks like a participle, but if you look closely at the sentence, you will see that it is the direct object of "forsaking"; it is what we are not to forsake. Grammatically, "assembling" functions as a noun here.) Bible markers may want to mark participles with (a), (b).

Just for fun, if you'd like to try your hand at picking out other passages' participles to see how they can enhance your understanding, check out Matthew 28:18-20 and Ephesians 5:15-21.

> If part of how we are to consider our brethren and stimulate them toward love and good deeds is by not forsaking the assembly, what, logically, happens to our brethren when we do forsake the assembly?
>
> Again, logically, if being in as many assemblies as we can be is part of how we provoke one another toward love and good deeds, what kinds of conversations should we be having when we're assembled together? Should our "fellowship" conversations revolve around clothing, shoes and sales on groceries? Or should we be talking about things a bit deeper, more spiritual than that? List a few ideas of conversation topics that would stimulate someone else on toward love and good deeds.

We're to encourage each other "all the more as [we] see the day drawing near." We don't have enough context to tell what day exactly is being referenced. It could be the destruction of Jerusalem, the day of assembly (as in Sunday), or it could be the day of Jesus' return. None of the interpretations change the meaning of the command: encourage, encourage, encourage, and then encourage some more!

In chapter three, when we studied Hebrews 3:12,13, you were asked to make a specific plan to encourage your brethren, write it in your calendar, and carry it out. How did that work? Whether it went well or not, it's time to do it again! Encouraging should be a way of life. So, let me ask again:

What, specifically, will you do today and tomorrow to encourage your brethren? Make a plan including a time to carry out your plan. Mark it in your calendar and be sure to follow through!

Remember: encouragement is part of how we keep ourselves and others from hearts hardened by the deceitfulness of sin.

Read Hebrews 10:26-31.

Here is yet another warning for all of us, and this one is a bit more lengthy. We're told that if we continue sinning willfully, there is no sacrifice left. The word for "willfully" appears only here and in 1 Peter 5:2. Elders are to serve voluntarily and intentionally, not because they were forced. Here, if we sin voluntarily and intentionally on a continual basis, there simply isn't a sacrifice that will cover that. Jesus' flesh was the ONE perfect sacrifice. If we reject that, we're out of luck; there is nothing else that will do the job. It's like the song says: "What can wash away my sins? Nothing but the blood of Jesus." And if there isn't a sacrifice to cover our sins, we stand as an enemy of God, and there is only terrifying judgment to look forward to. In essence, we choose which promise we'll take part in: the promise of judgment and fury of fire, or the rest promised beforehand.

The Hebrews writer has proven beyond a doubt that the new covenant is indeed better than the Law of Moses. If those who rejected the Law were killed without mercy, how much more deserving of punishment are those who reject this far superior covenant? Doing so is to trample the Son of God as a swine would pearls (cf. Matthew 7:6), to treat the sacred blood of Christ as though it were an everyday, common commodity, and to outrage the Holy Spirit who gave this grace. We know it was God who said in Deuteronomy 32 that vengeance is His, God who promised to repay, and God who also promised to judge His people. The same God who is the faithful foundation of hope is also a faithful foundation for expectation of terrifying judgment. He is no stone god to be mocked. Rather, He is the living God.

The portion of this section which is of utmost importance to us comes from Hebrews 10:26. "…after receiving the knowledge of truth…" This "receiving" isn't in-one-ear-out-the-other. It is the word we see in Hebrews 7:9 for Levi receiving tithes. Do you suppose that those tithes were given a quick glance then returned? No, of course not. Some would say that this strong warning given by the Hebrews writer does not apply to true Christians, for true Christians could never fall away. It simply isn't true, though. This warning is given to those who have received, accepted, taken in the knowledge of the truth. This warning is for us.

Take a moment to check yourself. Is there a sin to which you are clinging? One you just aren't "ready" to give up? Whether it is small or large in comparison to others' sins doesn't matter. Whatever sin you continue to commit will cause you to lose the only sacrifice, the only covering there is now or ever will be. Make your choice: terrifying expectation of judgment or hope of rest?

Read Hebrews 10:32-39.

In Hebrews 4:11, the writer gives a warning, then an encouragement in Hebrews 4:14-16. In Hebrews 6:6-8, he warns again, then encourages again in Hebrews 6:9ff. We find this pattern here too. We've had the warning, and Hebrews 10:22-29 is the encouragement. In some ways, this is a preview of Hebrews 11, so we won't spend too much time here. He reminds them of their faithfulness after they became enlightened. While it's clear this is a reference to their conversion (which has strong implications when considering Hebrews 6:4), "enlightened" may seem at first a strange word to use; we often think of enlightening as a word belonging to religions such as Buddhism and Hinduism. Not so, though. It speaks of light shining into darkness and illuminating it. Isn't that a perfect picture of what Jesus, the true light (John 1:9), does? In turn, we become the light of the world (Matthew 5:14). These Christians have been enlightened and now they must decide to hold fast rather than throw away their confidence (Hebrews 10:35).

The writer says that what they need is endurance, HYPOMONE. From here on, this is an important word, and one of which Bible markers will want to take note. It occurs in Hebrews 10:32, 36; 11:25, 27; 12:1, 2, 3, 7. It is "the capacity to hold out or bear up in the face of difficulty."[16] Envision a soldier on the front lines holding his ground even under fire, and you have the picture. This is the quality they need so that when all is done, they will receive all that was promised. The soldier who deserts receives none of the spoils, but the one who endures receives his reward. Just as there is no pleasure in a soldier who deserts or shrinks back, so God has no pleasure in those who shrink back from the faith. Shrinking back results in destruction. The writer is once again assured of better things for these Christians, though. He says "we are not of those who shrink back…but [we are] of those who have faith." It is as though he is saying we're not on that team over there, the destruction team. We're on THAT team, the faith team, the winning team, and he's about to introduce some of the other teammates, the men of old (Hebrews 11:2). What a team it is! Our fellow teammates are Abel, Enoch, Noah, Abraham, and the list goes on. Our list of teammates is better than the Dream Team!

Chapter 11

Better Than the Dream Team

When teaching this passage, it is tempting to get off onto a review of these people's lives and tell their stories all over again. That is not the point of the Hebrews writer's inclusion of them, though. His point is to show what true faith looks like, to remind his readers what it means to press on even when things seem bleak. If we are of those who do not shrink back, but instead are of those who have faith, we need to know what true faith is. These men and women are presented as models for us to follow. They are our fellow soldiers, our teammates.

As you read through Hebrews for this lesson, watch for "faith." Bible markers, if you haven't already marked "faith" as a key word, this would be the time to do it! Tracing the author's vision of faith through the book will especially help in understanding this chapter's import. In the New American Standard, "faith" and its derivatives occur 39 times, 26 times in chapter 11 alone. In your marking, be sure to include Hebrews 4:3 (NASB "believed") and Hebrews 11:6 (NASB "believe") as well as the times we find "faithful." Note that words in the NASB written in italics are not found in the original language, but are there to aid in our understanding. Personally, I mark these occurrences also.

Something else for Bible markers to consider doing is to look up the corresponding OT passages for each account mentioned in this chapter. If you have a cross-reference Bible, this can often be found in the references, but be sure to double check.

Read Hebrews 11:1-2.

Faith, like love, is a significant word in the New Testament as a whole. If 1 Corinthians 13 is the love chapter, this is the faith chapter. There is a caution here, though. Do not use the definition of faith from Hebrews 11 to sit in for all other places the word "faith" is used. Just as the word "love" has a different meaning when I say "I love hot dogs" versus when I say "I love my husband," so too "faith" can have a different meaning from one scripture to another. We abuse the text to attempt a one-size-fits-all definition.

There are things unseen, undetected by the senses, but faith is fully convinced that they are there. The promised rest we are to receive, Heaven itself, is not visible to our eyes or tangible to our hands, but those of us with faith are convinced of its reality. All that we hope for is as substantial to us as if we were holding it in our hands. This is what faith is. Faith moves one past doubting and into confidence. Certainly we are not the first to have this kind of faith, and neither were those to whom the Hebrews exhortation is written. Men of old, who will be detailed in the chapter, ran before with their faith as conviction and thus gained approval. From whom did these heroes gain approval? Men? Certainly not. They gained approval from God Himself. Denny Petrillo puts it this way: "Beginning with Abel and going through the myriads of individuals who filled the centuries, God always notices (cf. Hebrews 6:10-12). Those who moved beyond the superficial, and are able to develop a real faith based upon the abundant evidences supplied by God (cf. Romans 1:18ff) are those who receive this divine approval."[17] Faith is not blind. We have been given ample evidence in the creation which surrounds us. Based on this evidence, faith itself then becomes further evidence of what is to come.

Read Hebrews 11:3.

The first "by faith..." is referring to us. It is through faith that we understand and accept that God created everything, and did so with only His word, His command that it be so. To understand is "to comprehend something on the basis of careful thought and consideration."[18] Again, faith is not blind. Faith considers the lily of the field, the sparrow of the air, the fish of the sea, beast of the land and in thinking on it, sees that only an intelligent, loving superior Being could bring these to life. Faith asks, seeks and knocks, then finds the truth, and in finding becomes fully convinced that God did just as He said He did in Genesis: He spoke the worlds— both visible and invisible— into existence from nothing.

As a side point, consider what it means about someone's faith if they do not accept that God made the world of things which are not visible. Can one hold both a faith in God and a belief in evolution and/or science's other origin models?

Read Hebrews 11:4-7.

Our second "by faith…" refers to Abel. In the Genesis account of Cain and Abel, we are not told what exactly made Abel's offering acceptable to God while Cain's was not. Here, though, we have a clue: Abel's offering was of faith. Of course, the Hebrews writer's intent is not necessarily to enlighten us about Abel's gift, but to hold him up as an example. It is through acting on faith that he gained approval, and gained the testimony of God Himself that he was righteous. Not only that, but all these millennia later, he still speaks to us through scripture— all because of his faith.

From Hebrews 3:18-19, being disobedient is equated with unbelief (the opposite of faith). With this in mind, what may have been the difference between Abel's sacrifice and Cain's?

Enoch, likewise, speaks to us. While Abel lost his life because of faith, Enoch did not "see death" because of his. He, too, received God's testimony as pleasing to God.

Building on Enoch's example and the assumption that we will want to please God, the Hebrews writer tells us two prime ingredients of faith. What are these two ingredients?

The fourth "by faith…" is Noah. God told him it would rain and the earth would be flooded— two things never before seen (Genesis 2:6). He gave instructions for building an ark (something else likely not seen before) and Noah believed God. In reverence (can be understood as fear and awe), Noah did as God had commanded. His reward was the salvation of his family, the condemnation of the world which had mocked him, and the righteousness which comes by faith.

Read Hebrews 11:8-12.

Next up we have the faithful sojourners: Abraham, Isaac, Jacob and Sarah.

Abraham's faith is summed up easily: God called, Abraham obeyed.

Abraham, Isaac and Jacob all inherited the same promise, and gave up much in the hope of its realization (for your reference, Abraham received the promise for the first time in Genesis 12:1-3). Abraham left Ur, a city which is attested by archaeology to have been very advanced, and set out for a land he had not yet been shown. In the land, he and the two generations after him lived as though they were foreigners, strangers. God told him that the land would one day belong to his descendants, but during his life, his son's life, and even his grandson's life, it did not happen. It did not concern him, though, because he knew all things on earth, all things of men are transient and fleeting. He was more concerned with another city he had not yet been shown. He was concerned with the city whose foundations are not seen, whose maker is God.

Take a moment to consider what this was like for Abraham. For us today, it would be roughly the equivalent of living in a nice city with lots of culture and other perks, and then selling everything so we could go on a permanent tent camping trip to who knows where, somewhere we'll probably be digging our own potty. It took faith on Abraham's part! It also took faith on Sarah's part. We know from 1 Peter 3:5, 6 that Sarah was submissive to her husband. That would tell us she didn't grumble and complain (believe it or not, like it or not, a submissive wife is submissive in her attitude as well as her actions. I know, it's not easy for me either, but it is what God has called us to).

Hebrews 11:11 gives us some difficulty. For one, we quickly recall Sarah's laughter and subsequent rebuke when the promise of a son was given, so we see only her lack of faith. At the time when Sarah laughed (in Genesis 18:13), she and Abraham had been on their journey to divinely granted parenthood for over 13 years. Sarah had pushed her husband into another woman's bed, suffered mockery from her handmaid, and aged further all the while. The thought of a child in her own womb must have seemed entirely out of the realm of possibility.

Another difficulty we find is that the verse is variously translated in different versions. In such a case, it is best to let the original language clear away confusion. According to Petrillo, the subject of the sentence is still Abraham, not Sarah.[19] Martel Pace in the Hebrews volume of Truth for Today Commentary offers this possible translation: "By faith he [Abraham] also, together with Sarah, received power to beget a child when he was past age, since he counted him faithful who had promised" (453, 54). Pace also suggests that, like many of us, Sarah's faith grew in company with her husband's strong faith and was bolstered all the more by the conception and delivery of her longed-for son. This we know without difficulty: Sarah bore Isaac in faith and here we find her in the so-called "Role Call of the Faithful." Her laugh should not be cause for criticism from us, but rather a source of comfort: she who once laughed now stands as an example of faith. That being the case, there is hope for me, and hope for you.

> Can you think of a time when you've shown little faith? How have you worked to overcome that? How can you work further to overcome an attitude of laughter toward the promises of God?
>
> Read Hebrews 11:13-16.

Abraham, Isaac, Jacob and Sarah all died without seeing the complete fulfillment of God's promises. Abraham certainly received Isaac as part of the promise, but he never took possession of the land promised, and he never saw all the nations of the earth blessed by his seed. According to Galatians 3:16, that promise was only fulfilled in Christ. Though they never saw these promises fulfilled with their physical eyes, through the eyes of faith, each of these did see and welcomed them. This word for "welcome" means "to be happy about, to anticipate with pleasure."[20] Not only did they see these promises, they incorporated them into their very identity as though they were done. Sometimes I ask my son to do something and he says "Done!" meaning that he's going to do it, and he's going to do it now; I can consider it done. That's how it was for our faithful sojourners: God had promised, so they considered it done.

These pilgrims of faith could have turned in their tents and headed back for civilization at any time. God wasn't going to stop them or stand in their way. Some believe that we have no choice but to do God's bidding (a doctrine often referred to as "irresistible grace"), but even here we see that isn't how God works. God most certainly intended and wanted Abraham to leave Ur, yet the Hebrews writer tells us that Abraham still had a choice. Likewise, the recipients of the Hebrew exhortation had a choice. They could follow in God's laid out path or choose to return to their previous ways. Today we have the same choice. Will we look by faith and strive for a country of our own, even when it means we are strangers and aliens (both in the sense of being foreigners and sometimes in the sense of being downright odd)? Will we desire the better, heavenly country? If we do, then just as Christ was not ashamed to be called our brother (Hebrews 2:11), likewise God will not be ashamed to be called our God.

Read Hebrews 11:17-19 and Genesis 22:5.

This, to me, is one of the most amazing passages of scripture in the entire Bible. If you recall the story, God tells Abraham to sacrifice Isaac. You remember Isaac, right? Yeah, the one through whom all the promises were supposed to come. Now God says to kill him. Abraham knows God will keep His promise and He needs Isaac to do that, so Abraham just figures God will raise Isaac up from the dead after he's sacrificed.

In Genesis 22:5, he says, "I and the lad will go yonder, and _____ will return to you."

To you and I, his belief sounds like faith. Maybe it sounds sure, but not all that extraordinary, but consider Abraham's time. Had he ever seen anyone raised from the dead? Had he ever even heard of someone being raised from the dead? We have no Biblical reason to think he had ever heard of any of this. Noah had never heard of rain, but he believed God would do what He said (Hebrews 11:7). Abraham had never heard of someone coming back from the dead, but he believed God would do what He said, even if that meant resurrecting his son after being sacrificed. Wow!

Read Hebrews 11:20-22.

Isaac, Jacob and Joseph all kept their faith to the very end and instructed their children in living with a view to the fulfillment of God's promises. The Hebrews writer told his readers they were in need of endurance (Hebrews 10:36). That is exactly what Isaac, Jacob and Joseph had. Remember that the writer is painting a picture of what a faithful person looks like. Here we see that a faithful person believes God's promises even when no evidence is before his eyes, even though it sometimes takes longer than we thought, and even when his own life is ebbing away. Without faith, it is impossible to please God, and this is what faith looks like (Hebrews 11:6).

Read Hebrews 11:23.

Moses' parents saw that he was a beautiful child. We'd like to make this word mean more than simply physically pleasing, but that's really all it means. What mom doesn't think her baby is beautiful? Today's mom gushes about her baby's cuteness, and the dad shows him off proudly. So did Moses' parents.

Read Acts 7:20.

While the word we see in Hebrews 11:23 only refers to beauty, this passage says that Moses was beautiful in the sight of God, which is never based on external beauty (1 Samuel 16:7). Just as mothers (usually) think their children are beautiful, each child is beautiful in the site of God, whether born or unborn, loved or unloved, adored or not.

Moses' parents were emboldened to save him because of his beauty, but it was not this which enabled them to defy the Pharaoh for a full three months; it was their faith that made them unafraid.

What are some things you are afraid of happening if you exercise your faith fully, including sharing the gospel?

What consequence(s) were Moses' parents likely facing if they were discovered to be in defiance to the Pharaoh? Is it faithful or of little faith to fear the things you listed above?

Find out what Moses' parents' names were and, if you're a Bible marker, mark the reference in the margin of your Bible by Hebrews 11:23 (make sure you don't just google an answer without checking it!).

Read Hebrews 11:24-29.

Fill in this chart of Moses' choices.

Chose this ...	... instead of that
people of God	son of Pharaoh's daughter
	passing pleasures of sin
reproach of Christ	

Make a list of what Moses did by faith.

Read Hebrews 11:30, 31.

Moses chose God's people over Pharaoh's. Rahab also chose God's people. In fact, she chose to betray her own people because of her faith. She knew that God's people would conquer her city (Joshua 2:11). Her faith saved her and her family while those who were disobedient perished. Notice the contrast here between faith and disobedience. Faith that is not acted upon is not faith at all; it is disobedience.

Read Hebrews 11:32-38.

Find out who Barak and Jephthah are and what they did.
Barak:
Jephthah:

Which of these trials and victories listed sounds most amazing to you?

Read Romans 8:18.

Hebrews 11:38 says that the world was not worthy of them. In Romans 8:18, Paul says "the sufferings of this present time are not worthy to be compared with the glory that is to be revealed to us." Nothing in this world is worth, is of comparable value, to the reward that Moses wanted, to the country that Abraham desired. Faith sees that and acts on it.

Read Hebrews 11:39, 40.

All of these amazing things that happened throughout the history of man because of faith accomplished one thing: the approval and testimony of God Himself that they were righteous (Hebrews 11:4) and pleasing to God (Hebrews 11:5). These amazing, incredible, astonishing feats were done in faith, and what was their reward? They did not even have what we have! They were all looking to what we have now! If they can do all that without even having seen the fulfillment of the promise, we ought to remain faithful through far more.

Chapter 12

Finishing the Race

Let's jump right in!

Read Hebrews 12:1, 2.

The first word of the sentence is "therefore." This is not the usual word used; this is a particularly emphatic word, drawing the reader's attention with extra emphasis to this point. So what is the "therefore" there for? It's based on the whole last chapter's amazing definition and examples of faith. The Hebrews writer says "since we have so great a cloud of witnesses…" What witnesses? All those people in the last chapter. All those "men of old," those members of the "roll call of the faithful," our brethren! They are witnesses in that they are "those who have testified through their lives of faith that it can be done."[21] And they're surrounding us like a cloud. Have you ever stood in a cloud? You know those misty mornings when the ground is covered with fog? Every molecule of air seems to be bonded to one of water, and you can feel the very air. That is how thick, how numerous the cloud of witnesses is around us. And they're all cheering us on. Even when the voices here on earth fall silent and all seem to have abandoned us, these witnesses cheer on and on; we must remember that they are there and draw on their encouragement from beyond the grave. With their encouragement and their example, we can, we must lay aside those things which burden us and the sin that binds us.

> Read Acts 7:58, Ephesians 4:22-25 (esp 22, 25), Colossians 3:8, and 1 Peter 2:1. These verses all contain the same Greek word for "lay aside." Write down some of your observations/ thoughts about what this word means. Consider that in the first century people usually only had one or two sets of clothes; the chance to lay aside an old garment and don a new set of clothes would certainly be a big deal.

The word for "encumbrance" is only found here in the New Testament. It is a weight, or a burden. Notice that this word is describing something separate from sin. There are good things in which we can be involved, but those things may weigh us down. Remember too much of a good thing can become a bad thing. Women especially seem prone to becoming over-involved. In the church we have women who spend their talents and their time on jobs, clubs, committees, societies, and the list goes on. While these may be worthy pursuits, if they are standing in the way of doing the work of the Lord and His church, if they are not furthering the gospel and His kingdom, it's time to reevaluate! If you find yourself saying no when asked to participate in a work of the church because you just don't have time, that should be a red flag.

Think about what activities you are involved in and how you spend your time. List pursuits such as clubs, societies and hobbies, but also Facebook and other things that claim your time and attention (use another paper if you need to).

Read Matthew 6:33. What of your current time expenditures may need to be laid aside for the sake of the kingdom? Circle those activities above and start praying for God's wisdom as well as encouragement to back out of things that may be encumbrances in disguise.

Aside from encumbrances, we sometimes find ourselves caught up in sin. The Hebrews writer describes it as being entangled. The Greek-English Lexicon of the New Testament[22] explains that this word refers to something exerting tight control. Encumbrances and entangling sin combine to become like a ball and chain worn by prisoners in the past. They forced to wear those to keep them from running away, to keep them from pursuing freedom. That can happen to us! The Hebrews writer here urges us to cast away everything that weighs us down, tangles us up, and binds us where we stand. Then, the writer tells us to RUN. The word for "race" here is AGON. Does it look familiar? We get our word "agonize" from this word. If someone is agonizing over something, they are continuing to struggle over it, to put in both physical and emotional effort. Our race, our agonizing is against sin and for the kingdom with the promises of God bestowed at the end.

You may have noticed that runners don't usually run looking backwards or even to the right or left. They set their gaze and run. So it is with us. We must set our eyes, fix them, keep them steady on Jesus. He has crossed the line. He is the firstborn from the dead (Colossians 1:18), the first above all. He is the one who opened up the new and living way (Hebrews 10:20). He is the pioneer of our faith, the founder and originator (cf. Hebrews 2:10), and He stands at the finish line cheering on with the rest of the cloud of witnesses. He is, in fact, the most prominent of the witnesses. Just as they ran this race and endured, Jesus Himself ran and endured. He laid aside the luxury of Heaven, refused to be entangled in sin, set His eyes on the joy to be derived from saving mankind, and endured even the cross, shameful as it was, and received His promised reward, the highest of honors: the right hand seat to the very throne of God.

We've spent plenty of time on these two verses, but bear with me a moment longer as we put the whole picture together. This is an amazing passage of scripture because of the goose-bump imparting, tear-jerking, incredibly encouraging picture that is painted here.

Imagine the following scenario for a moment. Read it, then close your eyes and sear the image into your heart so it can spur you on in hard moments.

You're standing on a track in the middle of a stadium as huge as you've ever seen and it's packed to the gills with all-stars from every walk of life. The starting line lies before you and the crowd is a roar in your ears, everyone cheering for you. You reach down and unwrap your ankle weights, tossing them to the side. This is no training session. You check your laces and pull them tight, double-knotting them. Nothing will entangle you on this race, this most important run of your whole life. You set your feet to start and raise your eyes to the finish. The crowd roars on, and you see Him standing at the finish line, the one who loves you more than anyone else ever could. Jesus Himself is waiting, cheering, urging you on. You take a deep breath and the crowd jumps to its feet. As you hear their encouragement, as you see your Savior calling to you, the world, the worries, everything but THIS race, this moment fades to nothing. And you RUN.

Read Hebrews 12:3.

The Hebrews writer asks his readers to consider Jesus. Martel Pace explains, "The word for 'consider'… can mean basically to 'draw an analogy.' We can compare Jesus' suffering to ours in order to learn how to remain steadfast in the face of mockery and shame. Although 'despising the shame' and suffering, Christ focused on the greater joy of what He accomplished on the cross. We should think more about our benefits from the cross than about the temporary shame that may come from fellow humans."[23]

Read Galatians 6:9 and Luke 9:62.

Growing weary, and losing heart is a possibility, but we must endure. When our race gets difficult, we can remember the example set not only by the cloud of witnesses, but also the example set by Jesus himself. When we compare what we go through (especially here in America) to what He endured, it really isn't worthy to be compared to the glory to be revealed (Romans 8:18).

Bible markers, did you notice how many times "endure" and its relatives have appeared? It might be something you want to mark (note: in the NASB Hebrews 11:25, 27 have "endure/d" but these are not the same Greek words as the other occurrences; there are six total occurrences of the Greek word for endure). Also note the two occurrences of "let us" in Hebrews 12:1 and to mark those if you haven't already. Remember that this phrase has the same impact as a direct command.

Read Hebrews 12:4-11.

The Hebrews writer essentially tells his readers that what they're going through isn't that bad and to look at the bright side. It's not really something we appreciate hearing when we're in the middle of a pity party (valid or otherwise), but sometimes that kind of wisdom is just what we need. He reminds them that they haven't even shed blood yet. Recall from Hebrews 10:34 that they had suffered the seizure of their property, so their persecution is not small and more than I know of any American suffering. Some believe we may reach the point where persecutions of American Christians will be more outright, more physical, more difficult to bear, and they may be right. For the Hebrew Christians, they needed to buck up now because while they had not yet resisted to the point of shedding blood, there was no guarantee that it would continue that way. Likewise, we have no guarantee that our current, quite mild persecutions will not intensify. If we find ourselves whining about what we face now, how will we bear more severe difficulties? Sometimes what we face seems to be different from what they faced. Regardless of where our persecutions come from, we must remember the admonition given to the Hebrews. We must also remember the fruit of endurance (see James 1:2-4).

While some of what we endure may come from the world, the ultimate source may be God. With this perspective, we can count it a blessing, a sign of approval, a chance to be further molded to the likeness of Christ. Even when trials are anything but joyful, when they're sorrowful and threaten our faith, when we have endured through their training, we find the peaceful fruit of righteousness. We can once again imagine an athlete. Training can be brutal. Muscle growth comes from first breaking the muscles down so that they can be built up stronger than before. That does not sound like fun! That does not sound like a joy! But athletes endure because they know that when the training is done, their goal will be that much closer and their bodies that much stronger. When our faith is being challenged, it is a chance for it to be built back up stronger than before.

Read Hebrews 12:12-14.

The "therefore" here is based on the inevitability of suffering, trials and discipline of the Lord. Because discipline is sorrowful for the moment as well as inevitable, what should we do? He gives three commands or imperatives.

List the three commands.

We have two centers of focus given here: others and ourselves. There is a saying that goes with the acronym J.O.Y. (Jesus first, others second, yourself last) which can be misleading. One must care for themselves in order to care for others. The difficulty comes when our care for self and our care for others is out of balance. An over-focus on either can be extremely detrimental. The tricky part is that self-care doesn't take nearly so much time as we like to give it!

We are to strengthen the hands that are weak and the knees that are feeble. These are people who no longer feel they can do the work of the Lord and those who are weary of running the race. The command is to strengthen them. We are to be those who encourage and lift up. Consider what happens when Suzie, for example, shows up to worship. She hasn't been there in three months, and you're pretty sure whatever she's been doing isn't very godly. Now here she is and, what? What will happen? She's wondering what will happen too, and it probably took a great deal of courage to get there in the first place. She will feel more eyes on her than are even in the building, hear more whispers than anything else and wonder what everyone is thinking of her. Will she get the stink-eye everywhere she looks? Will she be questioned harshly about where she's been and what she's been doing? Or will she hear, "I'm so glad to see you! How have you been? I've been praying for you!" Or better yet, does she know that already because you've been contacting her? Will she sit alone or will you invite her to join you? Some say that Christians are the only army who shoots their wounded. This is sad, but all too often true. The good news is that one person can help to turn the tide. When the congregation sees someone kindly embraced, they are more likely to follow suit.

Who can you think of who hasn't been to worship in a while? List their name and make a plan of action. A simple card or even a text message may be just the thing they need to let them know you're thinking of them, that you care and they are welcome. Make a plan, then work the plan.

Read Hebrews 12:15-17.

Here we find yet another warning about the possibility of falling away. Some contend that it is impossible to fall from grace or that it is entirely out of our hands. Why would the Hebrews writer warn about something that wasn't possible or command them regarding something over which they have no control? That alone tells us the contention is incorrect. Additionally, the word for coming short has to do with failing to qualify. Think of it again in terms of athletic competition. If I want to compete in the high jump event at the Olympics, I must meet a certain standard, or I will not be admitted to the games as an athlete. Likewise, if we allow a root of bitterness, immorality, or any other encumbrance or entanglement to do so, it will keep us from qualifying. It will cause us to fall short of the grace of God.

Notice, though, that the warning does not say "see to it that you do not come short…" but that no one comes short (obviously within the realm of reason, we cannot force anyone to follow God).

"The Christian community has the responsibility to 'be their brother's keepers.' Otherwise they are no different than a godless person like Esau who was devoid of spirituality but instead was a man of the world. Esau sold his birthright, not considering it worth much. Are these Christians going to fall into the same mindset, considering their birth into God's family as worthless? Eventually Esau recognized the value of what he gave up. So also will these christians, who will find no repentance— or change— in God's judgment. Once that final day comes, all decisions are final" (Petrillo 62).

Read Hebrews 12:18-24.

On a separate paper, make a simple chart with one side listing the qualities of the mountain we have not come to (Hebrews 12:18-21) and the other side listing the qualities of the mountain we have come to (Hebrews 12:22-24).

Comparing the two charts, we see that the Hebrews writer has followed his pattern. He has issued a strong warning against falling away, but followed it up with encouragement. What a mountain we have come to!

Read Hebrews 12:25-29.

Here we have another warning, a command. If those of the Old Testament did not get away with rejecting Moses and the law he brought, can we really expect to get away with refusing to hear the very Son of God? Surely not. He shook the earth then (judgment terminology) and He's planning to do it again. This time, though, everything temporary—that is, all the earth and the heavens as well—will be shaken (cf. 2 Peter 3:10). When this second shaking happens, those things which are truly eternal will be revealed, and God's kingdom—our kingdom by His gift— will be revealed with it. That being the case, we ought to show gratitude, thanksgiving. This is how we can give pleasing service to God. We must bear in mind what kind of Deity we serve. Our God is no impotent god of the Egyptians who cannot even defend the Nile. No, this is the God of the universe, and He is a consuming fire. This quality makes it all the more important that we seek to render that acceptable service, that pleasing life to Him.

Chapter 13
Tips on How to Run

The closing of this exhortation to the Hebrews is full of gold. The writer has worked to convince his readers that they are right where they should be and that they must continue to run the race set before them. Now he moves on to practical instructions for their race.

Read Hebrews 13:1-3.

This general command covers so much! If we have true love for the brethren, what wouldn't we do for them? It serves as the basis of the next two commands. Interestingly, this is not the typical AGAPE love we see in the New Testament, but PHILADELPHIA (brotherly love). We are, of course, to have AGAPE (unconditional) love for our brethren, but there should also be a more intimate level of love between members of the Lord's church. Sometimes we hear people say "I gotta love 'em, but I don't have to like 'em!" The Hebrews writer would disagree. There is something likable in anyone. You may have to work to find it, and you'll certainly be closer with some brethren than with others (even Jesus had friends with whom He was closer among the disciples), but if you look, you can find something to like in everyone.

Part of showing love to the brethren is to have a home that is open to God's people. We are told here not to neglect, forget, or overlook this opportunity. And what an opportunity it is! To think of entertaining angels! "Abraham (Genesis 18:3), Manoah (Judges 13:3ff) and Gideon (Judges 6:11ff) all entertained angels. While some do not see the writer suggesting that this might still take place today, in view of previous comments (e.g. 1:14), there is no reason to believe that it can't."[24]

The word for hospitality is literally "stranger love." Of course, there are many ways to do this. It may not always be a wise idea to take someone into your home. Remember the command of Jesus to be innocent as doves, but shrewd as serpents (Matthew 10:16); we should be ready to serve, but must avoid naiveté. We can certainly show hospitality by putting a stranger up in a hotel, etc., but we should not be too quick to dismiss the idea of traditional, in-your-home hospitality! If you found out later that the man you'd put up in the hotel was really an angel, wouldn't you be kicking yourself? I know I would. Remember, too, that in context, we're talking about brethren. My family and I have been blessed many times to stay with families who were unknown to us, but well-known to God and His service. Our standing as fellow servants of the same Master meant that we were welcomed in His name. Whenever you have the opportunity to house someone, you would do well to take it!

This command is one that hit me between the eyes a few years ago. I'm a terrible housekeeper, and here I'm told to show hospitality? Me? Yes, because it isn't really my house, is it? If hospitality is a command, and I'm going to obey God, then the command applies to me now. While my house is a mess. While I'm still waiting for that dish fairy to show up with her buddy the laundry gnome. Not inviting people over isn't an option. So if my house is a mess, part of the price of my obeying God might be a bit of embarrassment. But you know what I've found? The people we have over usually care far less about the mess than I do (if they even notice it). We end up having a great time and that tie that binds grows stronger. In short, the love of the brethren continues. Another concern people have is cost; they're afraid it's just too expensive. Believe me, though, you can be hospitable on a shoestring.

Assignment: Get on Pinterest or Google and search for "cheap recipes for a crowd," or "cheap hospitality." If you're studying in a group, brainstorm inexpensive ideas for a gathering. Here are a few suggestions to get you started.

- Cereal potluck. Everyone brings a box or two of their favorite cereal. You provide the milk. You can even have everyone bring their own bowl and spoon. For some bonus fun, swap bowls and spoons for a unique souvenir.

- Just desserts. This is especially fun for after Sunday or Wednesday evening services. No need to serve a meal; just bring out some dessert or a plate of cookies and maybe some coffee.

- Beans and cornbread. This is just good ol' comfort food, and it sure is cheap.

- Hobo Stew. Everyone brings a can of their favorite soup and they all go in one giant pot. Yes, even the chowders. What's the worst case scenario? The soup is awful, and everyone has a good laugh.

- Stone Soup. Similar to Hobo Stew, each person brings an assigned soup ingredient such as carrots, onions, cooked ground beef, etc. Get your hands on a copy of the children's story "Stone Soup." When your crowd is assembled, have an old-fashioned read aloud of the book, then add the ingredients to the pot. This one could be a lot of fun for young families.

- Surprise dishless dinner. Get some plastic placemats from the dollar store and clean them well. Make up a big batch of spaghetti and when it's time to serve the meal, forego the plates. Serve directly on the placemats and watch your guests' faces. This is hilarious! You can be nice and give them silverware, or not!

Next we are told to remember the prisoners and ill-treated. This is like when you tell your child to remember the trash on Tuesday night. You don't mean for him to just think of it, but to actually take it to the curb so the trash truck can pick it up. This particular command can be difficult for us to apply today; we don't typically know anyone suffering in prison because of their faith or being beaten for the cause of Christ. Be on the lookout for people who may find themselves discouraged, lonely, and persecuted. Consider those in jobs who are surrounded by ungodly people all day. Consider those in the military and their families. One Air Force wife told me that she was often so lonely while her husband was deployed and she desperately hoped someone would invite her and her children over for lunch after services. For her, the hurt was so fresh that she cried as she told of her pain, even years later. Also, consider missionaries and what difficulties they may be suffering in God's service; a simple care package can mean a lot. Watch for needs, apply the golden rule, and take action.

Read Hebrews 13:4.

The word here for "honor" is elsewhere translated as precious (see 1 Corinthians 3:12, 1 Peter 1:19). If you have, for example, a ring or other piece of jewelry that is precious, you take care of it. So it should be with our marriages. God intended marriage to be a joy and a blessing. This only happens when we work to maintain a good relationship. Contrary to society's view, love doesn't just happen. Really, just about everything society teaches us about marriage is contrary to God's ideas about marriage. In society today, sex before marriage seems like a given, but the Hebrews writer tells us that fornication defiles the marriage bed. Fornication comes from the Greek word PORNEIA. It is the one reason Jesus gives for divorce (Matthew 19:9), but we must be careful. While the word looks like it would include pornography (which would then justify divorce if one partner engages in pornography), it does not. PORNEIA requires actual intercourse. "PORNEIA applies to a wide range of sexual irregularities, including sexual perversions as well as intercourse between unmarried persons, or between a married person and anyone other than his or her own spouse. Homosexual acts are condemned by this term."[25] While the viewing of pornography is not specifically condemned by this word, it certainly is not allowed by this passage or any other in God's word. No one could adequately argue that engaging in such an activity qualifies as honoring marriage. Also condemned here are those who engage in adultery. Adultery is going outside one's marriage for sexual gratification. Again, the actual act is what is being spoken of. The only holy, sanctioned, God-approved plan for meeting the natural sexual urges of mankind is within the marriage bond; anything else defiles the marriage bed and dishonors marriage in society as a whole. When marriage is dishonored, the family begins to degrade, and as the family goes, so goes society. Just look around America for evidence of this sad reality.

Assignment: If you are married, do something nice for your spouse. Bonus assignment: go to 5LoveLanguages.com and take the love languages test. Ask your spouse to do the same, then do something in keeping with his love language.

Read Hebrews 13:5, 6.

"Watch your thoughts, they become words;
watch your words, they become actions;
watch your actions, they become habits;
watch your habits, they become character;
watch your character, for it becomes your destiny."
-Frank Outlaw

If we are to keep our character free from the love of money, we must start with the root: our thoughts. We must actively strive for contentment. "This passage is talking about a person's attitude. Love is an attitude of choice, and so is contentment. The Christian has to make the right choice."[26]

Read 1 Timothy 6:8-11.

What, according to Paul is the bare minimum for contentment?

Sometimes the best way to stop one habit is to cultivate a new, better one. If discontent is ruling in your heart, you can use Paul's prescription in 1 Timothy 6. What does he say to pursue?

Read Philippians 4:11-20.

Many claim Philippians 4:13 as their favorite verse, but what is the true context of this encouraging verse?

The Hebrews writer comforts us and encourages us toward contentment with the knowledge that we always have God. Again, remember from Hebrews 10:32-34 that these Christians had already lost belongings because of their faith. Perhaps a little love of money was a motivation for returning to Judaism. With a return, they could avoid persecution and once again have the things that they felt they missed. But the author encourages them that if they have God, they really have all they need. With God on our side, there is nothing man can do to us (cf. Romans 8:31ff).

Just as a side note, did you see that God is here referred to as a "helper"? In the Old Testament, we read that woman is made for the purpose of being a helper (Genesis 2:18). In that passage, the translators of the Septuagint (the Greek translation of the Old

Testament, completed in the 3rd century B.C. and likely used by Jesus Himself) used the word BOETHOS. Here God Himself is said to be a BOETHOS. We must conclude that for woman to be man's helper is not derogatory in the least.

Read Hebrews 13:7.

This seems to refer to leaders who had since passed on to their heavenly reward, their reward being the result of their conduct. The word for leader is a general, but strong one. This does not necessarily refer to an elder or apostle, but definitely someone who did more than lead by example. This is someone who spoke the word of God and continued until death. These people were worthy of emulation and imitation. We often have those in our lives whose conduct and faith we can admire. We ought to cherish their example after they are gone and during their lifetime.

Read Hebrews 13:8.

This is such a popular passage! In context, it is a comforting one as well. The same Jesus, who rewarded those leaders who spoke to the Hebrew Christians, will also reward the one who imitates their faith. This includes the original readers as well as us.

Consider also what comfort this verse could bring to those who had faithfully served as Jews and who were now serving as Christians. What a change this was! And a change God Himself had brought about. Would He be changing things up again? No; in fact, Jesus was the same, is the same, will always be the same. This change was always the intent; it was the original vision. There would be no further change. Christ's sacrifice was "once for all" (Hebrews 7:27, 9:26, 10:10).

Read Hebrews 13:9-13.

Hebrews 13:8 proves an excellent bridge. Since Jesus is the same, we ought not think that His teachings will change. The Jews had special laws regarding foods, and so did the Gentiles. Jesus, though, declared all foods clean in Mark 7:19. The word for "strengthened" here is also found in Hebrews 2:3 and is translated there "confirmed." The Christian's heart ought not to be confirmed or strengthened by his/her own works or conformity to law. Rather our hearts are to be strengthened by the grace which we know rests in the sacrifice of Christ. Those serving in the Temple were only serving a tent, the shadow of the reality and had no right to eat from the altar where the Christian derives so much: the sacrifice of Jesus.

"On the Day of Atonement the animal sacrificed was not to be eaten by the priests, but instead was a burnt offering— that is, it was totally consumed (burned). Also, in a symbolic gesture, the animal was burned outside the camp, representing the removal and destruction of the sins of the people...Jesus is the ultimate fulfillment of the Day of Atonement. And, to further the type-antitype, the author points out that Jesus was killed outside the gate (cf. John 19:20), demonstrating the fact that He was rejected by the Jewish nation and sent without to die. However, He is the sacrificial Lamb of God, and those who want forgiveness will have to reject Judaism and go to Him outside."[27]

Read Hebrews 13:14.

There must be a good reason and a handsome reward for someone to give up their family and their religious heritage in order to follow a condemned criminal who was killed on a cross when the Jewish leaders demanded it. But the Hebrews writer reminds them that to do otherwise is to choose what is temporary over what is eternal. Jerusalem would only stand a few more years before being destroyed, many people's blood staining the streets.

Where else in Hebrews did the writer speak of a Heavenly city?

Read Hebrews 13:15-16.

Relying on grace and having no sacrifices at the temple could leave one feeling listless, uninvolved, even lazy. But there is plenty for us to do to please God. We have our own kind of sacrifices to offer up. Just as Abraham laid Isaac on the altar, we continually offer praise. The writer calls it the fruit of our lips. The fruit is the useful part of a plant. It's the reason a farmer grows his corn, the reason we plant an apple tree, the reason we care for tomato plants in the summer. The praise and thanksgiving of our lips is the fruit of our lips. It is what our mouths should be about. Oh, how often our mouths are used to complain, gripe, even tear down, and gossip! What blighted fruit that is! Along with the fruit of our lips, we have the opportunity to offer up good deeds and to share with others.

However, a sacrifice must cost the offerer something, right? And so too ought our praise, our good deeds, and our sharing. If nothing else, it requires time and a heart of devotion. Think again of Abraham. Ultimately, what did his sacrifice of Isaac cost him? He did not pay money, but it did cost him time, and it certainly required his heart of devotion. Like Abraham, our sacrifices must cost.

Read Matthew 25:34-40.

What are some sacrifices you can make? Brainstorm ideas here.

Read Hebrews 13:17.

The word for "leaders" is the same word as seen in Hebrews 13:7, 24. However, the context here would seem to indicate we are talking about elders. In a day and age when elders (if a congregation even has them) are seen and sometimes act as cruise ship directors rather than battleship commanders, the imperative of this verse is needed so very badly. Elders are those who keep watch over the very souls of their flock! This is no easy task and certainly not one to be taken lightly! If there were "varied and strange teachings" (Hebrews 13:9) less than 50 years after Christ's death, consider what our elders face today. We ought to do all that we can to make their job joyful and rewarding instead of one filled with grief. Do we squabble over the temperature of the auditorium? Or bicker over decorations of a classroom? Really? Aren't we adults? Figure out a solution to your problems, and put others before yourself (cf. Philippians 2:3). Watch for what the elders do well and encourage them about it. Bring them a plate of cookies or a card. Whatever you do, though, keep in mind the great charge they have and pray for them.

Read Hebrews 13:18-19.

The author requests prayers for himself and his companion(s), knowing that whatever they have done has been done in righteousness, though it seems others have accused him of wrongdoing. There are times in our own lives when we are wrongfully accused. Even when we know we have acted honorably and our conscience is clear, it hurts. The solution is (as it is for so many things) to rely on God through our own prayers and through the prayers of His people. The author's request for prayers is one of great importance and urgency. He wants to be restored to them, whether in the body or in a spiritual sense for the readers to return fully to the Christian faith. He clearly cares greatly for them even in his absence.

Read Hebrews 13:20-21.

Do you ever read a passage and think, "What a God we serve!"? This is one of those passages for me.

Fill in the chart below

Used blood for raising Jesus	Gave blood for eternal covenant	Received eternal covenant
	God works through Him	Equipped for every good thing
Works in us	Glory is His forever	Equipped to do His will
		God works in us
		Do works pleasing in His sight

Read Hebrews 13:22-23.

No doubt this was not a fun message for many of the readers. There were some hard truths that some even today refuse to accept. The author here urges them to bear with it, that is, to accept it as true and valid, and to receive it. Though the letter may not seem brief to us, there is so much more that could have been written. He is hoping to see them soon with Timothy and surely will encourage them further at that time.

Read Hebrews 13:24-25.

These final concluding notes remind us of letters and notes that we may have received as well. Grandma writes and finishes her letter with "Say hi to your sister for me." A friend writes and her letter concludes with "Suzie says to tell you hello." They wish us well and sign off. It is good to remember that the writer and those who received this exhortation were all just people just like us, trying to do their best to serve a God who strikes us with awe.

May grace be with us as well. And may we strive for the eternal reward so that we may one day all meet where there are no tears, and we can be with the Great Shepherd as well as each other for eternity in that city whose architect is God. May God bless you, dear reader.

Now it's time to RUN.

.

Endnotes

Chapter 2

[1] William Arndt, Frederick W. Danker and Walter Bauer, *A Greek-English Lexicon of the New Testament and Other Early Christian Literature*, 3rd ed. (Chicago: University of Chicago Press, 2000).

[2] Simon J. Kistemaker and William Hendriksen, *Exposition of Hebrews, New Testament Commentary* (Grand Rapids: Baker Book House, 1953-2001). 72.

Chapter 4

[3] Petrillo, Denny. Page 16. *"A Study in Hebrews."* Workshop in the Word. April 28-May 1, 1999.

[4] Orbison, Guy. Page 22. *"A Study in Hebrews."* Workshop in the Word. April 28-May 1, 1999.

[5] Orbison, Guy. Page 23. *"A Study in Hebrews."* Workshop in the Word. April 28-May 1, 1999.

Chapter 5

[6] Orbison, Guy. Page 26. *"A Study in Hebrews."* Workshop in the Word. April 28-May 1, 1999.

Chapter 6

[7] Petrillo, Denny. Page 34. *"A Study in Hebrews."* Workshop in the Word. April 28-May 1, 1999.

[8] Arndt, William, Frederick W. Danker and Walter Bauer. *A Greek-English Lexicon of the New Testament and Other Early Christian Literature.* 3rd ed. Chicago: University of Chicago Press, 2000.

Chapter 7

[9] Petrillo, Denny. Page 38. *"A Study in Hebrews."* Workshop in the Word. April 28-May 1, 1999.

Chapter 8

[10] Orbison, Guy. Page 40. *"A Study in Hebrews."* Workshop in the Word. April 28-

May 1, 1999.

[11.] Orbison, Guy. Page 42. "*A Study in Hebrews.*" Workshop in the Word. April 28-May 1, 1999.

Chapter 9

[12.] Orbison, Guy. Page 45. "*A Study in Hebrews.*" Workshop in the Word. April 28-May 1, 1999.

[13.] Arndt, William, Frederick W. Danker and Walter Bauer. *A Greek-English Lexicon of the New Testament and Other Early Christian Literature.* 3rd ed. Chicago: University of Chicago Press, 2000.

[14.] Orbison, Guy. Page 47. "*A Study in Hebrews.*" Workshop in the Word. April 28-May 1, 1999.

Chapter 10

[15.] Orbison, Guy. Page 48. "*A Study in Hebrews.*" Workshop in the Word. April 28-May 1, 1999.

[16.] Arndt, William, Frederick W. Danker and Walter Bauer. *A Greek-English Lexicon of the New Testament and Other Early Christian Literature.* 3rd ed. Chicago: University of Chicago Press, 2000.

Chapter 11

[17.] Petrillo, Denny. Page 52. "*A Study in Hebrews.*" Workshop in the Word. April 28-May 1, 1999.

[18.] Louw, Johannes P. and Eugene Albert Nida. *Greek-English Lexicon of the New Testament: Based on Semantic Domains.* electronic ed. of the 2nd edition. New York: United Bible Societies, 1996.

[19.] Petrillo, Denny. Page 54. "*A Study in Hebrews.*" Workshop in the Word. April 28-May 1, 1999.

[20.] Louw, Johannes P. and Eugene Albert Nida. *Greek-English Lexicon of the New Testament: Based on Semantic Domains.* electronic ed. of the 2nd edition. New York: United Bible Societies, 1996.

Chapter 12

[21.] Petrillo, Denny. Page 60. "*A Study in Hebrews.*" Workshop in the Word. April 28-May 1, 1999.

22. Louw, Johannes P. and Eugene Albert Nida. *Greek-English Lexicon of the New Testament: Based on Semantic Domains.* electronic ed. of the 2nd edition. New York: United Bible Societies, 1996.

23. Pace, Martel. *Hebrews.* Searcy, AR: Resource Publications, 2007. Print, 515.

Chapter 13

24. Petrillo, Denny. Page 65. *"A Study in Hebrews."* Workshop in the Word. April 28- May 1, 1999.

25. Pace, Martel. *Hebrews.* Searcy, AR: Resource Publications, 2007. Print, 559.

26. Petrillo, Denny. Page 66. *"A Study in Hebrews."* Workshop in the Word. April 28- May 1, 1999.

27. Petrillo, Denny. Page 67. *"A Study in Hebrews."* Workshop in the Word. April 28- May 1, 1999.

CPSIA information can be obtained
at www.ICGtesting.com
Printed in the USA
JSHW031345190322
23962JS00004B/89